ON ROMAN ROADS WITH ST. PAUL

ON ROMAN ROADS WITH ST. PAUL

By

R. MARTIN POPE

WIPF & STOCK · Eugene, Oregon

Wipf and Stock Publishers
199 W 8th Ave, Suite 3
Eugene, OR 97401

On Roman Roads with St. Paul
By Pope, R. Martin

ISBN 13: 978-1-5326-3504-5
Publication date 6/16/2017
Previously published by Epworth Press, 1939

Of the Jews five times I received forty stripes save one.
Thrice was I beaten with rods,
Once was I stoned,
Thrice I suffered shipwreck,
A day and a night have I been on the deep,
In journeyings often,
In perils of rivers,
In perils of robbers,
In perils from my countrymen.
In perils from the Gentiles,
In perils in the city,
In perils in the wilderness,
In perils on the sea,
In perils from false brethren.
In labour and travail,
In watchings often.
In hunger and thirst,
In fastings often,
In cold and nakedness,
Beside those things which are without, there is that which presseth upon me daily, anxiety for all the churches.

2 Cor. xi. 24–8.

Paul by reason of jealousy and contention marked out the prize of endurance. After that he had been seven times in prison, had been driven into exile, had been stoned and had been a preacher both in the East and in the West, he won the noble renown of his faith, in that he had taught righteousness to the whole world and had reached the farthest limit of the West. And when he had borne his testimony before the rulers, so he departed from the world and went unto the holy place, having become a mighty example of endurance.

Clement of Rome, Epistle to the Corinthians, V, (*c.* A.D. 95).

CONTENTS

LIST OF ILLUSTRATIONS

NOTE.—I am indebted to the courtesy of the Cambridge University Press for the views of Plate 12(*a*) and Plate 18(*b*), which are from Dr. Leaf's book, *Strabo on The Troad.* For the photographs of Asia Minor, Macedonia and Greece, I am most grateful to my friends Lieut.-Col. C. M. Turner, R. Gaddie, E. W. Harvey and F. W. D. Donaldson. I am also indebted to the staff of the Epworth Press for their valuable co-operation.

INTRODUCTION

'The gospel was first preached under an Anatolian sky . . . we are accustomed to read it under a northern sky.' So wrote Deissmann in his *Light from the Ancient East*, using the geographical term to cover not only Asia Minor but also Syria and Palestine, and it appealed to him as conveying to his mind the splendour of the dawn (or day-spring, the Greek *anatolê*). Literally, for him—and his readers—the sparkling and quickening sunbeam of the East reanimated the apostles and evangelists and brought out with greater distinctness the august figure of the Redeemer while it made ruined walls and buildings, stone and potsherd to speak. The present writer felt the power of that vivid experience and longed to share it. Three months before the close of the war the opportunity came, and even then I hardly realized what lay before me when I arrived at Salonika, henceforth, if a recent decree is unaltered, to be known by its former title, Thessaloniki. Here I was to feel the authentic thrill of the Near East and to spend six months within reach of Macedonia and Thrace, in a city which figures in the story of St. Paul as one of the important Christian centres established by his work: and subsequently to reside for six months in Asia Minor, first in the Troad and next on the shores of the Sea of Marmora. There the way opened to go farther afield on the track of St. Paul and to take a journey into Asia Minor as far as Konia, leisurely and unhurried, enabling me to alight at wayside stations, as well as to stay for some days at centres like Ismid, Eskishehr, Afium-kara-hissar and Konia. The sojourn might have been longer, but for trouble which had arisen at Smyrna between Turks and Greeks. This was a severe disappointment, for I much desired to travel through a region which, with Ephesus as the great Christian stronghold, fills a notable place in early Christian history and includes the churches of the Lycus, Colossae, Laodicea and Hierapolis, and the others associated in our minds with the Apocalypse. The general impressions of the whole year have been recorded elsewhere,[1] but at the suggestion of my friend, the editor of the Epworth Press, I have used these experiences, which brought me into close contact at many points with the journeys of St. Paul, to provide for the general reader an account of his adventures on the roads of the Roman Empire. It is not a life of the apostle,

[1] *Here and There in the Historic Near East* (Epworth Press, 2*s*. 6*d*).

a study of his theology, an analysis of his epistles or a fresh attempt to deal with the rather elusive problems arising out of the difficulty of harmonizing the history of the Acts with the statements of the epistles. These have been the themes of many Pauline studies, commentaries, and critical works during the last forty years. If I may be allowed a personal testimony, my interest in St. Paul began when, as an undergraduate, I read Lightfoot's Commentary on the *Epistles to the Colossians and Philemon.* The apostle's personality, his environment so swiftly changing in his active life, his letters, their Greek style as well as their content, his patience under incredible oppositions and rebuffs, his singlemindedness, his mysticism, his visions, his belief in divine guidance, his sublime courage—these and other aspects of his character and career made perhaps a more powerful appeal than the method and form of his doctrinal argument, which in detail suggested his Rabbinic training, and was inevitable in his effort to enlighten and convince his fellow-countrymen of the superiority of the gospel as contrasted with the law. Many to-day—and not unreasonably—have been prejudiced against features of his thought due to his ancestral training, and have revolted from their perpetuation in Christian theology. But on reflection, it is clear that only as a Jew could he have accomplished the task which he set himself to fulfil. From his ancestry and training he had learned the worth of the moral inheritance of Judaism and its place in the divine order of history and he now sought to show how its real consummation was to be found in a new creation, the redemption of the individual and humanity as a whole wrought by God in Christ reconciling the world to himself. To this object he devoted his strenuous, adventurous career, some aspects of which the following pages may serve to elucidate.

Among the numerous studies on St. Paul which have appeared in recent years, the place of honour by common consent is to be assigned to Professor W. M. Ramsay, whose works have thrown a wonderful light on the relation of early Christianity to the Roman empire. His *St. Paul the Traveller and Roman Citizen*, *The Cities of St. Paul*, *Pauline and other Studies*, *Luke the Physician* and other works have enabled hundreds of readers to understand the Pauline world, the geography, topography, archaeology of Asia Minor in particular, and its religious and political history. All students who attempt to expound the life, journeyings, available records of St. Paul's career and those parts of the Roman Empire in which his work was done, gladly acknowledge their obligation to his many-sided scholarship and none more sincerely than the present writer. His article on 'Roads and Travel' in Hastings' *Dictionary of the Bible*, and the geographical articles in the *Dictionary of the Apostolic Church*, by him and Dr. J. Strahan are most useful to the student of the N.T.

We are then to accompany the Apostle on his travels, beginning with the memorable journey—the second of his great missionary tours—which brought him from Asia to European soil, noting as we proceed from place to place in his itinerary the scenery, the historical and religious associations of locality and district and the results of his labours for the gospel. Probably our distinction of 'continent'—the difference between Asia and Europe—did not mean for a citizen of the early Roman Empire what it has come to mean for us of to-day. To reach Rome was Paul's secret desire. The dream of Christianity as a world religion took shape within his soul. It transcended all distinctions of place and culture and privilege. It was open to barbarians who knew neither Greek nor Latin, even to Scythians who represented the lowest scale of humanity. All human needs were fulfilled in Christ: and the unity of the Empire was an auxiliary to the accomplishment of the Divine purpose. The very roads ministered to the same end. They were all Roman roads. Not that Rome had made them all. Some went back to immemorial antiquity like the road from Ur of the Chaldees across the Syrian desert to Damascus, or the central and coast roads of Palestine itself which lead to the Sinai peninsula and to Egypt. The road system of the Empire enabled the Imperial government to communicate with the remotest countries, even the inhabitants of Britain on what appeared to be the edge of the civilized world. While the postal system established by Augustus to facilitate the delivery of state-correspondence was carried out by official couriers, the correspondence of the private citizen, conveyed by the hands of friends, was equally secure as depending on recognized routes of transmission open to the world.

Finally it may be stated that Prof. Ramsay's theory, which identifies the 'Galatians' with the inhabitants of the southern or Lycaonian region of the province of Galatia, was confirmed in my judgement as unassailable by actual study of the topography of that part of Asia Minor, while a visit to Angora, the ancient Ancyra and now known officially as Ankara, brought home to me the difficulty of finding a place in the extant records of the apostle's life for the evangelization of a district so remote from the Syrian Antioch or Tarsus. The opportunity indeed came to him at Dorylaeum but it was to the west and not the east that there his course was providentially deflected.

CHAPTER 1

THROUGH THE CILICIAN GATES TO LYCAONIA

In the year 49, three travellers had entered the great plain in which the city of Iconium lay. Their aim was to proceed from that city in a north-westerly direction towards Antioch in Pisidia and thence through Apamea, along the central route to Colossae and Laodicea, where they could turn north-west towards Smyrna or travel direct by Tralles and Magnesia to Ephesus. They were engaged on the adventure of preaching the gospel in the province of Asia, and on a journey the issues of which they could not foresee and in the course of which their plans were to be mysteriously changed.

But who were the three? The leader of the group and the eldest was a Jewish Rabbi known as Saul by his fellow-Jews, but named Paul by Greeks and Romans. Formerly an ardent Pharisee who hated and persecuted the new sect of Nazarenes, he had undergone a wonderful and complete spiritual change which had transformed his personality and opened before him a new calling in life. For nearly ten years after this conversion we have but scanty information about his movements but the greater part of this period appears to have been spent in his native city, Tarsus in Cilicia. Antioch in Syria had superseded Jerusalem as the centre of Christian life and movement in Palestine, and after these silent years of preparation for his life work we find him at the Syrian Antioch, summoned thither by Barnabas, to become his colleague in the ministry of the Church in that city, and to bring relief to their brethren in Jerusalem during a great famine. Paul was not only a sympathetic helper of the poor and suffering, but he was an outstanding teacher of the law and doctrine of Judaism, and a learned interpreter of the Old Testament, the Bible of his day, which had been translated from its original Hebrew into Greek two centuries before, and had been circulated all over the lands bordering on the Mediterranean. He could speak in that language as well as write in it with a style all his own, vigorous and if sometimes, through haste, grammatically rough and unpolished, yet with a rich vocabulary with which he could on occasion create a noble literary prose such as the hymn-like praise of Love in 1 Corinthians xiii. He could speak Aramaic, the dialect of Palestine, as he did before the crowd in Jerusalem, but Greek was his usual medium of teaching and preaching. He had imbibed in the atmosphere of the University at Tarsus a knowledge of Greek literature and thought, and had listened to the travelling lecturers, finding perhaps more to stimulate his thought in the tenets of the Stoics than in other forms of current philosophy. He was also a Roman citizen—a privilege he inherited from his father, which gave him a status of much value in his many-sided experiences, as affording exemption from bodily punishment when convicted before a local magistrate, and the right of appeal to the Emperor on the charge of treason. He had already proved himself to be a man of boundless courage and endurance, forbearing and tactful, while unswervingly loyal to conscience and the will of God as revealed to him in Christ. While physically equal to the strain of exposure to normal and even extraordinary conditions of travel, he quotes the judgement of his critics that while 'his letters are weighty, his person when present is feeble' (2 Cor. x. 10), without resentment, though with a quietly ironical hint against the danger of self-confidence and self-commendation, and later recounts the perils of his career in a moving passage (quoted above), which discloses many more risks of his life than we gather from our records. He suffered from 'a thorn in the flesh'—perhaps a tendency to epilepsy, malaria or an eye trouble—which was a continual source of distress. Whatever may have been his physical disabilities, he had a commanding personality, and by the intensity of his devotion to 'truth as it is in Jesus', by his unwavering belief that Christ alone could save mankind, and by his determination to preach Him 'in season and out of season', won many souls to righteousness and the kingdom of God. No one ever deserved the prefix 'Saint' more justly, and if we speak of him simply as 'Paul' in these pages, we have to understand it all the time, as we do in reading the New Testament.

He had with him Silvanus (Silas is the shorter Greek form), also a Roman citizen and a Christian 'prophet' or expounder of the faith, of whom we first hear as an outstanding figure at the Council of Jerusalem commissioned along with Paul and Barnabas to announce their decrees to the brethren of the Syrian Antioch

(Acts xvi. 4). He is now the chosen associate of the apostle and is with him throughout the journey as far as Beroea, where he is left along with Timothy, the third member of the group.

Timothy (Timotheus) is a youth who had joined the travellers at Lystra where his father, a Greek, and his mother, a Jewess, resided. How and where he was converted to Christianity we do not know, but his heritage of Jewish piety from his grandmother, Lois, and his mother, Eunice, united with his promise as a Christian, marked him out for the work of the ministry. Circumcised by Paul in order that he might be admitted without question to the synagogues of the Jews, he was the latest recruit for evangelical service and became to Paul 'a beloved son'. Though naturally of a retiring disposition and perhaps not physically robust, he was now to do the work of an evangelist. Only a few hours before, he had said farewell to his parents, and he was on the threshold of a new career in which, as we know from the letters sent to him by the Apostle, he was destined to fulfil his early promise and undertake with marked success important service in the ministry of the gospel.

Here for the moment we must leave them in order to record some details of the journey already accomplished by the two elder members of the group. They had started from the Syrian Antioch, the most famous of all the Antiochs,[1] a brilliant and attractive city of open spaces and wooded gardens, on the banks of the Orontes, the metropolis of Syria and known as 'the beautiful'. Its very site to-day, owing to changes wrought by earthquake, can only be partially determined. Syria, the narrow strip of country lying between the mountains and the sea, was at the point where, from a remote antiquity, the routes from Mesopotamia and Arabia have converged, and is fitly called by Belloc 'the Battleground'—the title of his recent historical study of this enthralling land. It was the city which coined the name 'Christian', perhaps in scorn or jest but usefully, as distinguishing Christians from Jews. It was now the chief centre of Christian activity in Palestine, and for centuries it was to be the source of evangelical movements and enterprise in Mesopotamia and beyond the limits of the empire, the inspiring genius and authoritative

[1] In addition to the Pisidian Antioch (Gr. *Antiocheia*), there was another on the Maeander in the province of Asia and two others of no great importance. The word was formed from Antiochus, the name of more than one of the Seleucid kings.

head of Syriac Christianity which produced one of the earliest versions of the Gospel—the Harmony of the Four (*Diatessaron*)—in Syriac, and later on an edition of the New Testament containing the Gospels, the Acts, and the Epistles of St. Paul in the same tongue, which was a branch of Aramaic. But Antioch was also the metropolis of Cilicia, the country bounded on the north-west by the Taurus range and stretching round the coast-line of the Gulf of Alexandria (Alexandretta) to Tarsus. The road which Paul and Silas took to Tarsus crossed the Amanus range at a point known as 'the Syrian gates' and then followed the coast-line to turn due west to Tarsus; it was familiar to him from the days of youth because it was the only road to Jerusalem and therefore associated with all the formative and critical events of his career from the day when as a pupil of Gamaliel he entered upon the study of the Law to the last visit when he was arrested by Claudius Lysias, tribune of the Roman guard, and sent to Caesarea to be examined by Felix, the procurator of Judaea.

Tarsus (Tersous) to-day, like Antioch, is but a shadow of its former magnificence. It was built on the banks of the Cydnus about ten miles from the coast. Now the Cydnus is half a mile away to the east of the town, which is without any interest but that of its rich, historic associations. Its port, Mersina, lies near the outlet of the Cydnus into the gulf. Tarsus itself lay on a wide plain less than a hundred feet above sea level, by no means a healthy or exhilarating site for a great city. Yet a great city it became in course of time through the energy of its people, who by engineering skill regulated the Cydnus, drained the surrounding plain, and made the city an inland port secure from the depredation of pirates. It was first the residence of a series of Oriental kings. Xenophon mentions as king of Cilicia Syennesis, who, with his queen, welcomed Cyrus at the outset of his expedition with the famous ten thousand Greeks in 401 B.C.[1] A hundred years later, after the conquests of Alexander, it became a self-governing Greek city, with a colony of Jews. Ramsay considers that in Tarsus the Hellenic and Semitic elements combined more successfully than in other great cities. This was an atmosphere which had a powerful influence on the mind of Paul, born and educated in a community, 'no mean city', where the rights and duties of citizenship were

[1] See *Anabasis* Book I, 2, which describes the route of the army from Sardis over the Taurus to Tarsus.

constantly making their appeal to him and subtly tending to form a sort of religious ideal, afterwards to find expression in his conception of the life of a Christian as a heavenly citizenship. Tarsus, finally, was a city of great importance as holding a strategic position in the province of Cilicia. Cicero, greatest of Roman orators, had resided there when governor of the Province and there Antony met Cleopatra for his first interview with her—an event of tragic moment for the fortunes of Rome. Its proximity to the 'Cilician Gates', which Alexander and many another military leader had entered in the course of operations in Mesopotamia and on the route to Egypt, added to its celebrity. Here, like Kipling's Mithraic soldier, a Jew might say 'Rome is above the nations but God is over all'—not, of course, the invincible Sun-god, but the God of Israel; while to Paul, Rome was a power ordained of the only wise God, God of all the nations revealed in Christ.

But before commencing the study of Paul's journey, let us attempt to answer the question which must have already occurred to my readers —How did Paul and his companions travel? Was it invariably on foot? We conclude that this was his custom, but it does not preclude the possibility that a horse or a mule may have been provided by his friends for shorter journeys in an area like that in which the south Galatian churches were situated, or in the neighbourhood of towns like Ephesus or Corinth. Some of his hosts like Gaius (Rom. xvi. 23) were given to hospitality, and Paul singles out this virtue as an essential to the Christian. But as a rule he went on foot, and though journeys in winter were avoided, and indeed on certain routes, like the Taurus mountain crossing, were impossible, it is clear that, whether on land or on sea, he faced the hardships with resolute and uncomplaining endurance. In the impressive passage in which he vindicates his claim at least to equality with other ministers of Christ, he specifies some of these hardships—actual hunger and thirst, sleeplessness and fasting, cold and insufficient clothing, the perils of desert country, and of robbers on the road. We can add to these the discomforts of crowded and unwholesome wayside lodgings or khans, for though with the traditional hospitality of the East no traveller in need would be denied a night's lodging, few of them could offer more than an unfurnished room, and food would be scanty if supplied at all. No doubt in certain parts of Asia Minor there were inns or hotels which offered excellent entertainment, but this was the exception and not the rule. A government official would find at each posting station or *mansio* relays of horses or even carriages waiting for him, but this only applied to those who had received an official *diploma* or permit. Seventy years ago, when the only railway in Asia Minor was the local Smyrna–Cassaba, the recognized method of travelling for those who did not use caravan or guides was to buy a couple of horses, one for riding and the other with a pack-saddle for luggage and a native servant. At the end of the tour the horses were sold. They put up at khans or public rooms in villages and thus could travel at the rate of two or three shillings a day. With a tent, an additional horse and a cook, according to Murray's handbook, *Turkey in Asia*, the traveller 'could be independent of all the world'. To-day Turkey is being rapidly modernized. Railways will soon cover the country; hotels, schools, hospitals and cinemas abound, even in the smaller communities. The old Turkey is gone for ever as the result of a régime not twenty years old![1]

[1] In 1923 I wrote that 'even the Nationalist party, if it abandons its militarist ideals and gives itself to the task of internal reorganization, may yet make out of Anatolia by

As to the rate of travelling in New Testament days, it has been calculated that the traveller on foot could cover from sixteen to twenty Roman miles a day (the Roman mile was 1,618 yards), but for the ordinary traveller sixteen miles is an excellent average, and probably represents the usual daily rate of travel.

From Tarsus to the Taurus range the road steadily rises for thirty miles, through vales watered by the Cydnus and in the shadow of impending craggy hills, until the famous pass of the Cilician Gates is reached. The track runs through a gorge which opens out on to the wide plateau of Asia Minor. 'The Gates', says Ramsay,[1] 'are a deep gap, worn by the Cydnus through a lofty wall of rock that runs athwart our path. Originally there was only room for a stream until the Ionian Tarsians cut out of the rock on the west bank space for a carriage road.' The road mounts higher to the broad pass called Tekir, 4,250 feet high. At this point the descent begins, over an upland region for many miles, before the

the help of the Western Powers a new and prosperous land', (*Here and There*, p. 151). This vision has now been realized beyond the dreams of imagination under the inspiring genius of the late Atatürk, President of the Turkish Republic.

[1] See *Pauline and other Studies*, pp. 282–3.

plain is reached and the traveller for the west arrives at Eregli (Herakleia which either is Cybistra or, as Ramsay thinks, near it). Forty miles to the north-west from this place, where there is a station on the Anatolian railway, lies Iconium.

But Paul must first visit Derbe and Lystra and to do so turns in a south-westerly direction, as the line does to-day, to Karaman, which is the modern name of Laranda, a once important city and metropolis of Southern Lycaonia. A striking feature of the landscape is the mountain called the 'Pilgrim Father' which looks down on the plain, where, near the two villages of Possola and Losta, lies the site of Derbe. Here, two years before, on his first missionary tour, the Apostle made 'many disciples' (Acts xiv. 21). Next to be visited was Lystra, where Paul and Barnabas had a remarkable experience. The site of Lystra has been identified as near the village of Khatyn-serai, twenty-five miles to the north-west of Derbe, on the great Roman Imperial road to Pisidian Antioch. The surroundings of the site of Lystra are pleasant, among low hills, with quiet gardens and a fertile soil kept green, as Ramsay says, by a water supply 'unusually lavish for the Lycaonian land', and like Beroea, a refuge of peace. Here the two apostles had arrived when the whole city was gathered for the annual thanksgiving sacrifice to Zeus (Jupiter) and Hermes (Mercurius), the messenger and spokesman of the supreme deity. The inhabitants were Greeks, educated and of social standing, and native Lycaonians speaking their own dialect. The city was governed by a body of Roman *coloni* who spoke Latin, but on this feast day they are not in evidence. When Paul had called on a lame man to arise and walk, and when the crowd had seen the cripple instantly leap up and walk, there was a cry raised, 'the gods are come down in our midst in the likeness of men'. 'And they called Barnabas Zeus and Paul Hermes, because he was the chief speaker.' Possibly in the folklore of the locality there was preserved a form of the old Phrygian legend about an aged couple called Philemon and Baucis who opened their humble cottage and provided homely fare to the two gods, Zeus and Hermes, who were travelling in disguise. Their rustic home was transformed into a temple by the grateful deities and the couple were made its priests. Their request that both might die at the same hour was granted and their bodies were changed into two trees which had grown from one root. The story has no connexion with the god of healing, Aesculapius, of whom Socrates, when about to drink the fatal cup, spoke to his friend Crito, bidding him pay the sacrificial gift he had vowed to that deity. But the reason is obvious. Zeus and Hermes were the patron gods of the city as Athena, goddess of learning, and the hero Perseus, slayer of the Medusa, were the patron gods of Iconium. That the historian who records this life-like and astonishing incident is strictly accurate is proved by a discovery reported in 1926 by Prof. W. M. Calder of an inscription on a limestone altar at Kavak, seven miles from Lystra, which runs, 'to the god who listens to prayer and to —— and to Hermes, a vow'.[1] The gap after 'and to' may be exactly filled with three Greek letters (the dative case of Zeus), or Zeus may be 'the god who listens to prayer' (*epêkoos*). Lystra had been granted the rank of a *colonia* by Augustus in 6 B.C., and of this there is proof in the basis of a statue of the Emperor found among the ruins of the town, 'the one direct reminder of the position of Lystra on the map'. But to return to the story. The impression made by the cure of the lame man was such that the priest of Zeus brought

[1] Quoted from an article in the *Manchester Guardian*, June 19, 1926; sub-title, 'A Discovery at Lystra'.

oxen and garlands to the gates of the temple before which an altar stood. Paul and Barnabas were horrified at the preparations of a sacrifice in their honour, and rent their hair and clothes, protesting that they were but human and that the Deity was living, not dead like the images to which he pointed, and was creator of the world, who never had left himself without witness, and whose beneficent purpose to all his creatures was seen in the harvest gifts and gladness.

Unhappily the good work begun at Lystra had a grievous sequel. Stoned nearly to death by the fickle crowd who had been instigated by the Jews, bitter opponents from Iconium and Antioch, Paul in company with Barnabas retired to Derbe. But not to surrender their task. Their experiences in Iconium and Pisidian Antioch will be referred to later. Suffice it to say that they had originally landed from the Syrian Antioch at Perga and had come over the Pamphylian highlands to the Pisidian Antioch, thence to Iconium, and thence to Lystra, as just described; but from their refuge at Derbe they returned, undaunted by past rebuffs, to each of these three churches, where they confirmed the souls of the disciples, urged loyalty to the faith, and after prayer and fasting commended them to the Lord. They did more: they organized the group of Christians in each place, by appointing elders over each (Acts xiv. 21–8).

It was probable that these events took place in the years 46–7. They returned by the way they had come, proceeding by the Pisidian Antioch to Perga, and thence by sea to their starting-place, the Syrian Antioch. It was the experience of the two apostles on this Lycaonian tour that strengthened their view, ultimately laid before the Council of Jerusalem, that the Gentiles henceforth must be received on equal terms with the Jews into the fellowship of Christians. Paul had no longer any doubt about the fatal consequences of yielding to the scruples of Peter and the Jewish Christians of Palestine in the matter of table fellowship with Gentiles, and it is not impossible that before the decision of the Council on hearing that in these South Galatian churches the extreme Judaists were continuing to 'bewitch' the brethren, he sent to the Galatians the first of his series of letters addressed to the prominent *ecclesiae* which he was to establish for the followers of Christ during his lifetime. He makes no mention of decrees in the Galatian letter, because he writes before they have been formulated. Against this view it has been held that the letters to Thessalonica which appear to be less mature in substance and style are the first he wrote; but these features may be accounted for by haste or circumstances which left him no opportunity for measured and leisurely composition, for they appear to reflect a situation that had suddenly developed.

No stirring incident, no events of moment occurred in the present visit to Lystra. Timothy, as already noted, joins the party. But it may be asked if it was just at this point that the Apostle was hindered by the Holy Spirit from going into Asia. Here he was on the imperial road leading direct to Pisidian Antioch and thence to Ephesus. But there is hardly any doubt that his thoughts were turning to the north, and that the three travellers took the road to Iconium.

Readers of the Acts (xvi. 1–6) will recall how the historian, after mentioning the visit to Derbe and Lystra and the joining of Timothy, reports that 'as they went on their way through the cities, they delivered them the decrees' . . . and that 'the churches were strengthened in the faith and increased in number daily'.

It cannot be doubted that among these Iconium and the Pisidian Antioch are to be included, although not mentioned by name. For the narrative continues 'they went through the region of Phrygia and Galatia', meaning by that description Phrygia-Galatia, or the southern end of the *provincia Galatia* as contrasted with the northern region of the province which was the old or original province of Galatia. If not accepted by all scholars, this is the view which has been largely adopted by recent commentators of the *Acts* following the lead of Professor Ramsay, its original exponent.

CHAPTER 2

ICONIUM, ANCIENT AND MODERN

WHILE Derbe and Lystra are vanished cities, Iconium (the modern Konia) remains. It is remarkable in legend, in history and in its natural features and surroundings. It ranks with Damascus as one of the world's oldest cities. Its name, Image-town from *eikon*, the Greek word for image, the ikon of the Orthodox Church of Russia and the Near East to-day, recalled the legend which made its site the scene of the creation of man, when Prometheus made images of clay, animating them by means of the fire he had stolen from heaven. Its site is on a vast plain 3,600 feet above sea-level, bounded by hills on the north and west, while on the east, distant summits rise like islands from the sea, and on the south-east horizon is the long ridge of the Taurus range. It was also the legendary scene of one of those great floods which figure in Babylonian traditions, but if this plain was submerged, the city was to rise again and become an important city of Phrygia and a centre of the cult of the Phrygian Mother-goddess, Cybele. Next under the successors of Alexander, the Seleucid kings, it became a centre of Greek life and culture, with Cybele superseded by Athena as patron goddess and Perseus as hero-god. In Paul's day it ranked as an outstanding Graeco-Roman city of the province of Galatia, later to become the capital of a new province, Lycaonia. From the age of Constantine under the Byzantine emperors, when Asia Minor was a Christian country, it achieved reputation as a stronghold of the Faith, where saints, like the virgin Thekla, and Amphilochius, its arch bishop, were venerated for generations.[1] During the First Crusade, Frederick Barbarossa achieved a memorable victory near Iconium, afterwards dying at Tarsus as the result of a bathe in the chilly waters of the Cydnus; and it is from the age of the Crusades that we date the rise of Islam which was eventually to transform Asia Minor from a Christian to a Mohammedan land. In the eleventh century Iconium was captured by the Seljuks, predecessors of the Ottoman Turks, who made the city the capital of the kingdom of Roum. Under their domination the learning,

[1] See Ramsay on the Orthodox Church in the Byzantine empire in *St. Luke the Physician*, p. 141 f.

arts, law and literature of Persia and Arabia found a home within its walls. In fact Iconium became a city so flourishing and splendid that it gave rise to the proverb 'see all the world but see Konia'.

But seen to-day Konia is disappointing. Though the plain of Konia as you enter it from the north-east suggests the barrenness of a desert, you find pleasant gardens of fruit trees, and shades cast by cypresses, within and without the city. Nevertheless, the general aspect of the city gives you an unhappy impression of neglect and untidiness. The dusty roads, the houses of mud-brick, some roofless and empty, the decaying mosques, the melancholy relics of Seljukian palaces, courts and schools ruined and crumbling, with only their lovely tiles of Saracenic faïence to recall their medieval beauty—such are the aspects that at once arrest and disillusion the visitor. Yet all is not lost of the interest and glory of a city which was once one of the most famous of the East. On the acropolis, a rounded eminence overlooking the city, though of no great height, you are reminded of Byzantine Christianity by the Christian church of St. Amphilochius, the archbishop of Iconium when it became the metropolis of Christian Lycaonia, and near at hand the famous mosque of the Seljuk Sultan Alau-eddin. Thence you descend into the bazaar from its bustle and heat to find refuge in the shade of the trees and by the fountain in the precincts of the mosque of the Mehlevis—a mystic sect of Islam with its presiding elder, the Kelebi, and its body of dancing dervishes. Neither the Kelebi nor the dancing dervishes will be seen again. The sect was suppressed by Kemal Atatürk, the first ruler of the new Turkey. But the buildings remain, owing not a little of their distinction to the cylindrical turret with its polygonal surface covered with tiles of brilliant green, the sacred colour of Islam. This marks the *turbeh* or tomb of one of the greatest of the mystics, the famous Jelalu-ed-din whose sacred poem, the Masnavi, is a classic of Islamic mysticism or Sufism. Its conception of God is purely pantheistic in that it regards the goal of all endeavour to be absorption into the all-absorbing love of the Deity. Yet its spiritual intensity is remarkable. You may open the English version of E. H. Whinfield and you will learn from the 'Song of the Reed' that God only is real.

> The Beloved is all in all, the lover only veils him,
> The Beloved is all that lives, the lover a dead thing,

implying that if God withdraws His presence from man, man is already doomed to die like a bird that has lost its wings. Here we discover how mysticism or the immediate awareness of God is the same thing wherever you find it, whether in a Christian or a Mohammedan. There lingers in the mind the recollection of a dimly lighted shrine with an altar-like tomb wherein lies at rest a singer who felt and expressed the love of the soul for God and the yearning for union with Him.

Iconium, when Paul visited it, had not as yet received the rank of a Roman *colonia*, but Claudius had given it the title of Claud-Iconium, thus officially recognizing its friendship with Rome. Nearly a century later, under Hadrian, it was made a *colonia* of the province of Galatia. Then, in 295, Diocletian created out of Galatia a new province of Pisidia, of which Antioch, next to be visited on this journey, was the metropolis; hence it became designated the Pisidian Antioch, while Iconium was held to be a second metropolis, occupying a central position towards the east on the highway to the Euphrates and on the road to the Cilician gates and Palestine. Of Paul's second visit to this city and Antioch we have no details, nor of a possible third

(Acts xviii. 23). But we have full particulars of the Apostle's pioneer work for the gospel in both places (Acts xiii. 14–xiv. 7) and we have his personal testimony to the persecutions he endured; 'in Antioch, in Iconium, in Lystra' (2 Tim. iii. 11). The opposition which he and Barnabas encountered from the Jews in the Pisidian Antioch and Iconium is an eloquent testimony to the effect of their preaching, accompanied as it was by signs and wonders wrought by their hands. The city populace of Iconium was divided; but it was not till Jews and Gentiles with the cognizance and support of their rulers (not the city magistrates) made a determined assault with stone-throwing that the apostles fled from the city to Lystra.

But, as we remember, it was only a temporary storm. Later the apostles returned first to Lystra, then to Iconium and finally to Antioch (Acts xiv. 21–3), in order to place as we have seen (see p. 33) these three churches on a proper footing with a stable organization through the appointments of Elders in each place. This is a memorable result which is so briefly expressed that its importance might easily be overlooked. There is an election to office submitted to the judgement and approval of the brethren followed by fasting and prayer and the solemn commendation of the elders to the Lord in whom they had believed. Christianity was thus established in Iconium and through all the changes of time has persisted. The humblest forms of Christian worship and service which exist to-day in Asia Minor are related to these historic inaugural acts as the beginning of a spiritual movement which is still going on among the millions of the vast continent of Asia. If ever we are assailed by doubts about the future of Christianity in the East, we have to contemplate the achievements of Paul, the pioneer missionary of the faith, and recall his words to another Asia Minor church, the newly founded Christian fellowship at Colossae. 'The word of the truth of the gospel is come unto you, even as it is in all the world bearing fruit and increasing'. The hyperbole of a great visionary! we might be tempted to say, as we stand by him in these isolated little fellowships so far apart, yet almost immediately becoming aware of a divine unifying power that mysteriously linked them all together, the spiritual counterpart of that imperial system to which they all belonged, with its vast lines of communication, radiating from a common centre—Rome for the first three centuries and Byzantium for the next eleven—

until in 1453 a Mohammedan Sultan sat upon the throne of the Christian Caesars.

As we stand on the acropolis of Konia, and look in a north-westerly direction, we see rising out of the plain two conical peaks which bear the names of two Christian saints of the second century, St. Thekla and St. Philip. Thekla was the subject of a romance in the apocryphal *Acta Pauli* which contains a description of Paul as 'little of stature, thin-haired upon the head, crooked in the legs, of good state of body, with eyebrows joining and nose somewhat hooked, full of grace; for sometimes he appeared like a man and sometimes he had the face of an angel'.[1] The story (which is dated second century by critics) is a legend of virginity which Thekla, moved by the teaching of the apostle, desired to maintain for life, although she was betrothed. In the sequel, Paul was expelled from Iconium by an angry crowd, and Thekla condemned to be burned. But the fire took no hold on her and Paul had her removed to Antioch, where again she was condemned, this time to fight with beasts, and once more was miraculously saved. Finally she returned to Iconium and the story

[1] See *The Apocryphal New Testament*, M. R. James, p. 272 f.

ends thus: 'after she had enlightened many with the word of God, she slept a good sleep.' This is of course a pious romance, but it relates to an actual saint who in her day lived a holy life and was full of good works.

Philip is held by Ramsay to be the Apostle, not the deacon, one of the Seven (Acts vi. 5), but the father of four aged virgin daughters and one of the 'great luminaries' of Asia, according to Eusebius who is quoting from Polycrates, a second-century bishop of Ephesus. It is possible that Philip, who was buried in Hierapolis, visited Iconium on his way to Hierapolis and Ephesus; certain it is that St. Philip supplanted a pagan deity who was worshipped on the mountain near Iconium, named by the faithful after the apostle, though geographically known to-day as Takali Dagh. Curiously enough, Philip is also the subject of an apocryphal series of *Acta* in one of which his reception at Hierapolis is related.[1]

In the fourth century, Asia Minor was pervaded by Christian influence and the names of Gregory of Nyssa, his brother, Basil of Caesarea, and another Gregory, of Nazianzus, afterwards bishop of Constantinople, known as the Cappadocian fathers, stand out as landmarks in the history of

[1] See *op. cit.*, p. 448.

Christian thought. In fact, Christian churches were to be founded in eastern Asia Minor from the Black Sea to the Taurus and of course farther east in Mesopotamia, where the Syriac-speaking churches created noble traditions of scholarship and missionary enterprise. But with the rise of Mohammedanism in the seventh century the strength of Christianity declined. Arabian religion, art and culture came in the wake of Islam, and Asia Minor became a Mohammedan land and is so to-day. But Christian institutions still remain, and the influence of Christian civilization is demonstrated everywhere in the new Turkey. Religion is tolerated and the charity and enlightenment of Western Christian lands is exemplified on every hand. The progress of the last fifteen years is marvellous. Angora, a picturesque but squalid hill town at the end of the war, has been transformed into a modern city with magnificent buildings and all the amenities of a European capital. The advance is equally marked elsewhere. A new railway connecting the Black Sea ports with the Gulf of Alexandretta through Kaisari (Caesarea) and great roads for motor transport are being engineered in a land where travelling has always been slow and difficult. Modern hygiene and sanitation have been introduced;

schools and hospitals with the up-to-date equipment of Western countries are being built. Physical cleanliness and fitness are being encouraged by the introduction of gymnasiums and sports grounds. The difficult Turkish characters are superseded by Roman letters and have disappeared not only from school books but from the press and public notices. All are marks of a new future; but what about religion? All history proves that material and scientific advance which leaves unsatisfied the deeper needs of the soul will eventually come to an end. If the ceremonialism of the Orthodox Church were to be leavened by evangelical ideals and a passionate zeal for the moral transformation of the individual, we might see once more in Asia Minor the triumphs of Paul and the early apostles who brought to a pagan world a light of healing and regeneration that has never been utterly quenched. Islam is the dominating faith of the Turkish Republic, in numbers and influence, but the country has never been without the social and religious activities of Christianity since the days of the early missionaries of the Cross.

CHAPTER 3

THE MOUNTAIN CITY OF PISIDIAN ANTIOCH AND ITS NEIGHBOUR PHILOMELIUM

The road from Iconium strikes due north over the plain where travellers have frequently seen the mirage, an experience which befell me as I approached the city, for on looking back a great lake had suddenly formed, so realistic that I thought I must have been asleep when I had passed the place in the train. The hills reached, the travellers mount to the ancient city of Laodicea Combusta (Gr. *Katakekaumenê*), that is 'burnt', from the furnaces of iron ore for which the place was famous. To-day called Ladik, the city is reached after nine hours on foot from Konia and may have been their first lodging-place. About an hour before arrival they would reach a ridge which commands a magnificent distant view of the immense plain of Konia as far as the summits that look down on Derbe and Lystra. It may have been the last time Paul was to follow this route, and he might well be comforted in the retrospect of his visits to the three Lycaonian churches whose stability, so far as we can judge, was now assured.

Thence to Tyriaeum, the modern Ilghin, where Syennesis and his wife, Epyaxa, met Xenophon and the ten thousand Greeks with a gift of money to pay the troops, an event of the distant past but known to Paul as a citizen of Tarsus. Next to be reached, twenty hours after Ladik, was Philomelium, the modern Akshehr, unless indeed he had turned towards the north-west at an earlier point and crossed the foothills of the Sultan Dagh to the Pisidian Antioch. We shall return to Philomelium later, but in the meantime let us contemplate in imagination the site of Antioch, once a great city. Its actual site is a matter of conjecture, but Ramsay has located it at a short distance from the modern town of Yalowadj. It is a scene of utter desolation. It lies on an upland level towards which descend the stone-covered western slopes of the lofty Sultan Dagh, whose topmost ridge is whitened by snow even in the height of summer. Near at hand flows the River Anthios through a ravine to fall into the great double Lake Limnai fifteen miles away. Lakes are often to be found in Asia Minor at no great distance from mountain ranges like the Karalitis Limnê, which lies thirty miles west of Lystra, and the great lake to the east of Philomelium. Probably the site of Antioch was selected because of its strategic position, strong enough to withstand attack from Pisidian hill-tribes and having the advantage of a good water-supply. All that is left of this great city is a stone floor with a few isolated solid blocks, probably relics of a temple of the God Men. Wild and lonely though the site is, there are mountain pastures and fertile tracts watered by the river. We have already noted that these ancient Anatolian towns developed in similar historic stages, first as native settlements, next as communities, advancing after the conquest of Alexander to the status of civilized Greek cities with a body of free citizens, until at a later stage they passed under the provincial authority of Rome as *coloniae*. Thus, when Paul first visited Antioch, it was a Roman *colonia* like Philippi, and called Caesareia Antiocheia, with Roman *duumviri* and a small senate, and a number of influential Greek-speaking Jews who, according to Ramsay, exercised with other Greek citizens a powerful influence. Hence the population may be divided into four groups: (1) the governing *coloni* bi-lingual—speaking Greek and using Latin for official purposes; (2) Greek-speaking citizens with pagan beliefs, yet in many cases 'god-. fearers' attracted by the Jewish creed, if not as yet 'proselytes', that is, converts who had been circumcised; (3) strict Jews, many of whom may have received the rank of citizenship; and (4) finally, native descendants of the original settlers, though probably few in number.

Christianity was brought to this community by Paul when, accompanied by Barnabas, he opened here his campaign for the gospel which is described with such remarkable vividness in the Acts (xiii. 14–52). The report is detailed and full, marking Luke's sense of its importance as the narrative of the laying of the foundation of the first of the four Galatian churches. Paul appears in the synagogue, and gives his notable address which is an epitome of his subsequent letter to the Galatians, and is in effect the argument afterwards expanded into the form of a treatise in the epistle to the Romans. Addressing his audience as 'Men of Israel and ye that fear God', he places together the strict Jews, descendants of Abraham, and the seekers after truth who have come to honour and believe in the God of Abraham, and proceeds to make an appeal to history. (1) God chose Israel in order to make through His people a disclosure of His Being and Will as shown in His leadership acknowledged not only by prophet and priest, but by the people throughout the vicissitudes of their history, which was in fact a preparation for a Saviour. (2) John the Baptist, the last of the prophets, disclaimed the title of this Messiah or Anointed One and pointed to Jesus as the Saviour of Israel. Here Paul, as if thrilled by the wonder of his message, addresses the whole company as 'Brethren', thereby in a word blotting out all distinction of race or religious privilege, and declares that the Saviour, though crucified with the consent of Pilate at the instigation of ignorant rulers and people blind to the teachings of the Scriptures, rose from the dead. His resurrection is the proof of His Sonship and of His power to forgive both Jew and Gentile who believe in His name. He concludes with a warning against contempt and unbelief.

The effect of this discourse was so profound that on the next Sabbath 'almost the whole city' assembled to hear the Apostle. The jealousy of the Jews was aroused, they became bitter, and eventually Paul and Barnabas were expelled from the district and retired to Iconium. They had, however, succeeded in founding what was destined to become a powerful church composed of numbers of the God-fearers and even proselytes, and likewise Jews who were convinced by the doctrine of the Apostles. Not long afterwards, as we have already recorded, they returned, and by the appointment of Elders established their converts into a Christian ecclesia. On this second journey, having either earlier at Lystra or finally here abandoned the project of going to the province of Asia, Paul crossed by the mountain road with his companions to Philomelium, the modern town of Akshehr.

Beautifully situated at the foot of the Sultan Dagh in a pleasant valley watered by a mountain stream and shaded with trees, Akshehr has some notable remains of the Seljuk Age. There is a weather-worn turbeh, the reputed tomb of Mahmoud Seir, one of the Sultans, with a superb tower and ruined walls and arches of noble symmetry, the remains of a medresseh or college. There are other relics of Greek architecture indicating a Greek city of some importance in the Byzantine Age. To the student of early Christianity it is interesting as the site of the ancient Philomelium, where in the second century a Christian community existed, perhaps an offshoot of the Church of Antioch, owing therefore its beginnings to Paul. A letter from the Christians of Smyrna in the second century has been preserved in the document known as the 'Martyrdom of Polycarp' addressed 'To the church of God which is resident at Philomelium and to all the churches in every place of the holy catholic church and may the peace and love of God the Father and the Lord Jesus Christ be multiplied'. It is a moving and much-treasured recital of the sufferings and martyrdom of the Bishop of Smyrna who died on February 23, A.D. 155 in that city. Called on by the proconsul to swear the oath and revile the Christ in order to secure his release, the venerable and noble saint said, 'Fourscore and six years have I been His servant and He hath done me no wrong. How can I blaspheme the king who saved me?' The crowd cried, 'This is the teacher of Asia, the father of the Christians, the puller-down of our gods and teacheth numbers not to worship'. This was nearly a century after Paul had been beheaded at Rome.

But it is also at least possible that another great saint and martyr, Ignatius, Bishop of the Syrian Antioch, forty years before the death of Polycarp passed through this very place on his way to Rome to be thrown to the beasts in the arena. He had been ordered by Trajan to be taken as a prisoner to Rome, and he was accordingly sent under guard, without any of the consideration shown by Roman officers to Paul because Ignatius was not a Roman citizen. The details of his journey, which may have been partly by sea, are not known, but that he passed through Philadelphia to Smyrna is certain since that city is definitely named. From Smyrna he wrote letters to the churches of Ephesus, Tralles, Magnesia, Philadelphia and Rome, together with a letter to Polycarp and one to Smyrna, sent after his visit to that city, which contains the memorable saying: 'Wheresoever Christ is, there is the catholic church.' All are valuable as throwing light on the Christian churches of Asia and their inner life and organization in the second century. Of their evidence on these matters various views have been held, but there is but one opinion of the personality of this beloved bishop, his unfeigned love of Christ and his brethren, his courage —as witness his words, 'I am the bread-corn of Christ to be gnawed by the teeth of beasts that I may be found pure bread', his humility—did he not say 'I do not enjoin you as Peter and Paul did. They were apostles, I am a convict'?—and his serenity of spirit undisturbed by the ills of time.

Thus, the memory of three martyrs is recalled on this high road which bore through Julia (Ipsus) and Primnessus to Philadelphia from Philomelium. Paul, Ignatius and Polycarp—three builders of the Kingdom of God of whom the world was not worthy.

We lift our eyes unto the hills, these hills that have seen the rise and fall of cities, themselves unchanged and symbols of the transcendent and eternal. We hear the murmur of their waters and recall the lines of the Duddon sonnet:

> Still glides the stream and shall forever glide,
> The Form remains, the Function never dies . . .

But it is the road that summons to duty, to adventure, to life, the road formed as a mere track by the feet of primeval man, but now an artery of an empire that controls the world. Chaucer chose it to mirror the joys and sorrows, the follies and wisdom, the sins and virtue of medieval England. Bunyan used it to portray also as a pilgrimage the passage of ordinary simple folk through the perils of soul and body to a Celestial city. Here within a narrow space, bounded on either hand, we are aware of the fellowships of time, the millions for whom the march is over and the millions of throbbing, striving, friendly, hostile creatures who are with us on the track. Only one poet and he of the new world, Whitman, has sung *The Song of the Open Road* with a happy abandon and optimism which most of us will covet:

> 'Allons! after the great Companions and to belong to them!'

CHAPTER 4

ON THE NORTH ROAD THROUGH PHRYGIA TO DORYLAEUM

TWENTY miles from Akshehr the road passes Isakli at the entrance to the Caystropedion, a plain which gave its name to a city which cannot be identified, where the expeditionary forces of Cyrus halted for five days; and about the same distance is covered by the traveller before reaching Tchai (Ipsus Julia), the scene of a decisive battle which gave the empire of the East to Seleucus about 300 B.C., who thus entered on the sovereignty of the new Orient which Alexander had opened to Greek enterprise and commerce. It was this Hellenized Phrygia which Paul and his companions were traversing for the first time, so far as we know, and here instead of taking the road due north through Nakoleia to Dorylaeum they continued on the more frequented route by Primnessus to Akroenus, the modern Afium-kara-Hissar, a remarkable little town lying at the foot of a huge rock which rises perhaps eight hundred feet from the plateau in isolated ruggedness. Here the plain is some three thousand feet above sea-level, and from the summit of the rock you see Phrygia, stretching out towards the east, a landscape of fruitful plains, with the Sultan Dagh on the south, a mountain range which for fifty miles has towered over the valley from Akshehr. On the western side the view is shut off by the hill ranges which encroach on that end of the town. It is the junction for Smyrna to-day, and in Paul's day was on the route to Philadelphia (Alashehr), to which Ignatius was conducted on his journey. The name and outward features became familiar during the war as the place where British troops taken prisoners at Kut were interned.

We have remarked on the position of Afium-kara-Hissar as standing at the turning-point for Smyrna, the road to which passes through Philadelphia and thence to Sardis, at which place an overland route proceeds north-west to Thyatira, Pergamus and Adramyttium on the southern coast of the Troad. A glance at the map shows that from Sardis the other fork led to Smyrna, and thus we have accounted for five of the seven churches of the Apocalypse, that is

Smyrna, Thyatira, Pergamus, Sardis and Philadelphia. There remain Ephesus and Laodicea. Ephesus, it will be seen, lies about forty miles south of Smyrna at the end of the central route which runs from the Pisidian Antioch. Between these two main roads approached from the east are situated Colossae, Laodicea and Hierapolis, the three churches in the valley of the Lycus, a tributary of the Maeander. We know how interested Paul was in these churches from the letters to the Colossians and the Ephesians. The latter, which was a circular letter and may be that letter to the Laodicaeans referred to in Col. iv. 16, was certainly without the name of its destination, until 'in Ephesus' was inserted in the first verse of the letter perhaps because it was felt that so important a church, known to have been under Paul's immediate charge for nearly three years, should have one of his letters assigned to it. Now this geographical digression will enable us to throw light on that most interesting, if vague, statement, referring to his ministry (see p. 117) in Ephesus, 'all they which dwelt in Asia heard the word of the Lord, both Jews and Greeks' (Acts xix. 10), a sentence which has given rise to the theory that he founded the seven churches of Asia.

We have reached the heart of Phrygia, a wild, mountainous country of narrow valleys and gorges, cave-dwellings and rock tombs, a home of religions, mystic, ecstatic, and esoteric, and of superstitions crude and ill-balanced. All classical students recall the numerous allusions in Greek and Roman literature to the cult of Cybele, the Great Mother, typifying the fertility of nature, her head supporting a tower, sceptre in hand or driving a chariot drawn by lions, with priests, the Corybantes or Galli, who danced and shrieked to the sound of drums and cymbals in a wild frenzy. Also known as Ceres, goddess of Corn, she was the presiding deity of the mysteries of Eleusis near Athens; and as Rhea, inspirer of similar festivals at Rome, where even early in the second century A.D. in connexion with the cult was introduced the *taurobolium* or baptism with the blood of bulls—a feature of Mithraism, the worship of the Sun-God, another Eastern cult which was to become a serious rival of Christianity. It is therefore not wholly surprising that this land led to the first heresy of the Christian church; for here flourished the strange growth known as Montanism, from its founder, Montanus, who was originally an idol-priest, possibly of Cybele, was converted to Christianity in the second century and taught that the age of revelation was not over, and that under the dispensation of the Holy Ghost, the Paraclete, fresh signs of the divine activity might be seen. He himself was a prophet and two of his disciples, Priscilla and Maximilla, vowed to perpetual virginity, were said in ecstasy or trance to deliver divine messages and to have the gift of tongues. As a reaction from the formalism and rigidity of church order and routine, it had a powerful appeal for many, and Tertullian, one of the most vigorous and gifted of the early Fathers, ended his days as a Montanist.

Another feature of Phrygian religion was the cult of departed members of the family. 'The dead man becomes god, going back to the goddess-mother who bore him.' [1] Hence the sanctity of the tomb which becomes a miniature temple with the gravestone as the altar. Some of these are impressive, like that at Deuver on the way to Kutahia. The Phrygians were originally an obscure tribe which migrated from Europe, entered the Troad and established itself perhaps a thousand years before Christ. Under the Seleucid régime, the original language was displaced by Greek, though it did not die out until the

[1] See art. *Phrygians* by Ramsay, *Dict. of Religion and Ethics.*

third century A.D. According to Josephus large numbers of Jews, who as supporters of Seleucus had won honour, were settled in Phrygia and received 'privileges equal to those of the Macedonians and the Greeks', but relaxed in their strictness of life, and became susceptible to non-Judaic influences. Paul had to combat at Colossae a type of Judaism that had a certain affinity with Gnostic ideas, extreme asceticism, contempt of the material as essentially evil and a denial of the Incarnation. On the other hand, the liberalizing tendencies of the Jews served to attract large numbers of 'god-fearers' and to secure many proselytes to the religion of their fathers; and, as we have already noted, this element of the Greek population provided many converts for the Pauline churches.

Sixty miles north of Afium-kara-Hissar lies Cotyaeum (Kutahia) reached from Alayund by a branch of the Anatolian railway after a brief journey from the main line. The junction marks the commercial interest of Kutahia in the sale of a local pottery. It is pleasantly situated in a fruitful valley, on a stream shaded by tall overarching trees amid scenery and in a setting which appeared to be not unlike that of a small English town in the hill-country of the north. There is a walled acropolis with the ruins of a Byzantine church, from which you look over bare rocky hills on all sides. From here the road goes in a north-easterly direction until in fifty miles Dorylaeum (Eskishehr) is reached, the well-known railway junction for Angora (Ankara) from Constantinople. It is an interesting centre because of its historical memories. North of the town a great plain stretches towards Ineunnu, lying at the foot of hills full of rock-caves and tombs. Here the First Crusaders in A.D. 1097 achieved a notable victory over the Seljuk Kilij Arslan which enabled them to penetrate southern Asia Minor, cross the Taurus and enter into Syria. Remains of the Crusaders are found on the hillsides of Eskishehr, a pleasant town on the River Pursak Su, the ancient Tembris, famous for the clay-beds from which meerschaum was made.

We have now reached a point in the journey where a number of problems arise. Hitherto all has been fairly clear. Preaching the word in Asia has been abandoned; but we have now to explain what is meant by the verse (Acts xvi. 8) which declares that 'when they were come over against Mysia, they assayed to go into Bithynia, and the Spirit of Jesus suffered them not, and passing by Mysia, they came down to Troas'. At the moment they were certainly over against Mysia, the most northern of the three territories of the Province of Asia, the other two being Lydia and Caria, bordering the Aegean on the western side of Asia Minor. Dorylaeum which they had reached, was, as we have noted, within the bounds of Phrygia, which is sometimes distinguished as Phrygia-Asia, in contrast with Phrygia-Galatia, which contains Antioch, Iconium, Lystra and Derbe. Here they were at a junction which north, east and west opened on lands that needed the gospel. Take the east, in which direction the road led to Ancyra (the modern Ankara), capital of the northern and older section of the Province of Galatia. Here Paul would have met the descendants of the first immigrants from Gaul, and further, might have visited Caesarea (the modern *Kaisari*), the capital of Cappadocia, afterwards a stronghold of Christianity, or proceeded north to Pontus—we remember that Jews from both these lands were present in Jerusalem on the day of Pentecost. But his mind was set on going north to the important Province of Bithynia, west of Pontus, its shores washed by the Black Sea, the Bosporus, and the Propontis (or Sea of Marmora). Here were the great cities of Nicaea (Isnik) and Nicomedeia (Ismid), the latter to be the scene of the first outbreak of the terrible persecution under Diocletian in 295 and, half a century after Paul, to be administered by the younger Pliny whose correspondence with the Emperor Trajan is a valuable sidelight on the life and worship of Christians resident there. Nicaea was to become famous as the city chosen for that first great Council of the Church which formulated the creed of 325, by which the orthodox doctrine of the person of Christ was defined. But the way to Bithynia was closed against him by the voice of the Spirit. There remained the west, and the west it must be for Paul. We are reminded of Wordsworth, greeted on Loch Katrine shore by the question, 'What, are you stepping westward?'

> And stepping westward seemed to be
> A kind of heavenly destiny. . . .
> The echo of the voice enwrought
> A human sweetness with the thought
> Of travelling through the world that lay
> Before me in my endless way.

CHAPTER 5

WESTWARD BY MOUNT IDA TO ALEXANDRIA TROAS AND THE AEGEAN COAST

'AND passing by Mysia, they came down to Troas.' We must now return to these enigmatic words already quoted. Do they mean that they skirted Mysia, the territory that lay between them and the Aegean? Unless they went by sea, this was quite impossible. They could of course have started in a north-westerly direction by a route that took them direct to Prusa (the modern Brusa), a city with a beautiful situation at the foot of the snowy Mysian Olympus, and boarded a coasting vessel at the port of Mudania, or have reached Cyzicus farther west, and sailed round by Lampsacus which is on the Dardanelles, opposite the town of Gallipoli, to Alexandria Troas. If they had landed at Lampsacus, they could have followed on foot the coast road past Nagara Point, Chanak, Kum Kaleh on the plains of Troy, and Yenishehr to Alexandria Troas. These are modern names of well-known points on this famous and beautiful road which is fa to readers of Homer and Herodotus; the supreme genius who gave the world 'the t Troy divine' in the *Iliad*, the other the fascir historian who narrates the expedition c Persians under Xerxes against Greece in 48(and the crossing of his huge army on a bri(boats from Abydos near Nagara Point. But a tive as this theory is, it must be dismissed as c ful on the ground that Luke, who has a m interest in all maritime details, coasting and voyages, ports and shipping, would have cer reported this incident. Further, he uses tl pression 'went down', which means in the or Greek going from the interior of a country coastline, the opposite of going up (*ana* that is leaving the sea. *Anabasis* is the ti Xenophon's History of the expedition of tl thousand Greeks, who became restive the f: they got into the interior, and had to be t and cajoled into submission to orders, unt crisis occurred which ended happily in 'going down' from Mesopotamia and rea the Black Sea, with losses that seem surpri small.

We are driven to the conclusion that 'p: by' in this connexion means 'passing ov(

'neglecting' the country, in the sense that they deliberately avoided making long stays for evangelistic work in the towns they visited on this journey. As a matter of fact, their route lay over a wild and, in certain parts, a trackless region, so far as we can judge; but for the most part the itinerary is a matter of conjecture. It seems probable that they would take a line by the left bank of the river Rhyndacus which rises in the Dindymos range of Phrygia and flows north-west into a lake close to the Marmora. Two other rivers flowing in the same direction, the Macestus and the Tarseus, have to be crossed and, as the map shows, two more, the Aisepus and then the Granicus, on the left bank of which Alexander won his first victory on Asiatic soil. Ramsay quotes a later tradition to the effect that, between the Rhyndacus and Cyzicus on the Marmora, Paul and Silas founded a church at a place named Poketos, and another tradition that a certain Onesiphorus, a martyr to the faith under Hadrian, when the latter was proconsul of Asia, evangelized a part of Mysia. How far these traditions are trustworthy is a matter of opinion, but it is difficult to believe that they do not contain a kernel of fact. Finally, Paul would take the road which led westward to Artemis

Thermaia, the hot springs, sacred to the goddess Artemis, on the River Aesepus. The cult of Artemis, as we may recall from the history of Ephesus, was popular in the province of Asia. The next stage is not easy to determine; but we are helped by the brilliant commentary of Walter Leaf[1] on the topography of the Troad as recorded by that early geographer, Strabo, who wrote his *Geographikon* about the year 7 B.C. From Strabo's statements we may construct the route of Paul and his companions as taking them in a south-westerly direction to the base of Kotylos, from which the road goes to Skepsis by way of the foothills of Mount Ida (5,800 feet high). Ida, as Strabo says, dominates the Troad with a series of ridges that are the main watersheds of the country. Skepsis is on the right bank of the Scamander, which flows due west by the modern Bairamich to Ezine, where it bends northwards to flow over the plains of Troy into the Hellespont. The road from Skepsis crosses the river almost immediately, and on its left bank reaches Ezine in about twenty miles. Ten miles farther to the west lies the site of Alexandria Troas, with its little harbour opening on the Aegean Sea.

There can be little doubt that Paul had read

[1] See his *Strabo on the Troad.*

Homer, who was to the Greeks what the Authorized version of the Bible is to an educated Englishman, but it is unlikely that he turned aside to see the plains of Troy and the Hellenistic city of Novum Ilium, the new Troy, of which a conspicuous feature was the marble temple of Athena. This site is about twenty miles away from Troas, near the village of Hissarlik. For a long period the site of Homer's Troy was assigned to a site among the limestone crags of Bunarbashi, several miles to the south of Hissarlik until Schliemann began, in 1865, to excavate the hillside on which lay fragments of fluted columns belonging to the vanished temple of Athena, being convinced that under the New Troy were concealed the remains of the Old Troy of Homer's Iliad. His belief was triumphantly proved to be correct. The whole achievement is a romance of archaeology. On the one hand, we have the life-story of this German scholar, who, when fourteen years of age, a miller's son and apprenticed to a grocer, heard a miller's man recite a hundred lines of Homer, became fired with the love of Homer and Greece and worked hard until he had saved sufficient money to come to the Troad and begin to dig on the famous hillside overlooking the plain of Troy. On the other hand, we have his achievement, the discovery of six settlements, afterwards shown to be really nine, lying in successive layers, until massive walls of the Mycenaean age, 1300 B.C., were revealed and found to be the remains of the fortress of the Homeric Troy. Within this fortress Hector and Andromache, Helen and Paris dwelt during the famous siege which ended in the sack of the citadel and its destruction by fire, though the foundations resisted total ruin and are visible to-day. Incidentally, Schliemann had established the belief of many scholars that there was an historic basis for the Homeric epic of Troy and that the legend was a picturesque setting of an actual struggle for the commercial freedom of the Dardanelles.

Mount Ida, Homer's 'many-fountained' Ida, was the haunt of the gods who watched over the fortunes of Troy during its ten years' siege and where (to quote Tennyson's *Oenone*)—

> The gorges, opening wide apart reveal
> Troas and Ilium's columned citadel,
> The crown of Troas.

By 'Troas' he means that district of the Troad which Leaf calls 'Troyland', and, as we have seen, it was in the vales and under the ridges of the mountain that the road to Alexandria Troas passes even to-day. It is remarkable that Strabo merely names the city, probably because in his day it was a modern town having no associations, like other places on the coast, with Homer's Troy and, as Leaf says, it was 'a purely maritime and commercial town' which owed its foundation to its harbour. Only remains of a theatre, baths built by Herodes Atticus, a munificent governor of the city under Hadrian, and other ruins are visible, and the whole site of this walled city with a circumference of six miles is neglected and overgrown with valona oaks. It was originally founded by Antigonus as Antigonia, but this name was changed to Alexandria after the battle of Ipsus referred to on page 57.

But interesting as these details are, they cannot, for the student of early Christianity, be so absorbing as the human interest of Luke's narrative at this point in the Acts of the Apostles. Hitherto on this journey we have had to rely on the evidence of the earlier travels of the Apostle to enable us to realize the conditions of Christian church life in the four Lycaonian cities of Phrygia-Galatia. But at Alexandria Troas an entirely new feature appears, a personal factor of the utmost importance. The narrative of the Acts changes from the third person plural to the first, indicating that the three travellers have been joined by another, the reporter. First comes the ever memorable passage: 'A vision appeared to Paul in the night; there was a man of Macedonia standing, beseeching him, and saying, "Come over into Macedonia".' Next follows the comment: 'And when he had seen the vision, straightway WE sought to go into Macedonia, concluding that God had called US for to preach the gospel unto them.' Who was this mysterious person? Was he a complete stranger or was he a friend of the Apostle? Or had Luke himself, whom Paul had met for the first time on arriving at Troas, so roused the apostle's mind with the suggestion of the need of Macedonia that, in a dream, this need embodied itself and took shape in the person of Luke himself? Much is to be said for the theory first put forth by Professor Ramsay[1] that the man of Macedonia was none other than Luke, who reports the vision. His case is strengthened by the peculiar formula, by which the stranger is introduced 'a certain man, a Macedonian'. It is, on the face of it, a not unpleasing artifice or literary device characteristic of the versatile genius of Luke. It is pointed out

[1] *St. Paul the Traveller*, pp. 202–4.

that in our earliest records Luke is named as a Syrian of Antioch, but this looks as if it were an attempt to give a definite form to the original statement of Eusebius[1] which means nothing more than that Luke was 'one of those in Antioch', that is, that he resided there, though really a Macedonian by birth. Macedonia had trading relations through its port at Neapolis with Troas and other ports, including Antioch, in the southern Aegean. The name Luke is the English form of Lucanus (Gr. *Loukas*, cf. Silas and Silvanus). It is agreed that he was a physician, 'the beloved physician' of the letter to the Colossians (iv. 14), a Gentile and a writer with a Greek style of his own marked by a certain literary finish and a sense of artistic fitness, not wholly enamoured of the Jews but with enlightened and broad sympathies, and a devoted Christian of the Pauline type. He shows a special interest in cases of sickness and bodily ailments as if he had some professional interest in, or even close knowledge of, medical terms, lending support to the tradition that he was a physician; he is extraordinarily accurate in details, e.g. local official titles (e.g. 'politarchs', 'Asiarchs'), and in nautical matters like the handling of a ship and

[1] Euseb, *Hist. Eccl.* iii. 4.

the technical terms of its equipment, and in his knowledge of navigation in the Mediterranean. It is at least possible that, but for this providential rencontre with Paul, we might never have had the third gospel with the parable of the Two Sons and other passages which take us to the very heart of the gospel, nor the Acts, an invaluable and unique record of early Christianity. He certainly was a notable convert to the faith who has laid the world under an imperishable obligation by his writings. But we will not dwell further on these qualities; they will shine by their own light as we continue to take him as our guide in the record of the memorable travels of the apostle.

The immediate result of Paul's meeting with Luke was to take ship over the sea and to visit Macedonia for the first time.

CHAPTER 6

ON THE VIA EGNATIA TO PHILIPPI AND AMPHIPOLIS

WHEN Julius Caesar crossed the Rubicon, it was to become master of the Roman world. But when Paul took the gospel to Europe, he laid the foundation of an empire of the Spirit—a *civitas Dei*—which while in the world, is not of it and will survive the fall of the kingdoms and cities of time. For the present, the faith of Christ was to be bound up with the imperial system of Rome. The East gave Christianity to the West; and when Paul and his companions, including a newcomer, Luke, landed at Neapolis, the port of Philippi, they entered the Province of Macedonia, which in 168 B.C. had become an important addition to the empire, inasmuch as Rome thereby had opened a corridor between East and West which has lasted till to-day. The Balkans have always been a kind of bridge between the two continents. The choice of Salonika as a base of operations in the Great War is a proof of this statement, and the victory of the Allied troops was an event which helped to settle the issue of the struggle on the Western front. Our troops that landed at Kavalla, the modern name of Neapolis, during the Salonika campaign probably were unaware of the historic significance of this ancient port. When Paul landed at Neapolis, he was the pioneer of a movement which through the imperial lines of communication was to affect the civilized world. It is therefore to us as it came to be to him also, a clear mark of providential guidance that he, a Roman citizen, should now visit Philippi and Amphipolis, two notable cities of this key province, and later proceed to Thessalonica, the seat of imperial government for the province as a whole.

'Setting sail therefore from Troas, we made a straight course to Samothrace, and the day following to Neapolis' . . . (Acts xvi. 11). He was following a recognized Roman route between the continents and doing it more quickly than on a subsequent occasion when it took him five days to sail from Neapolis to Troas (Acts xx. 6), no doubt owing to difficult conditions of wind and weather. They put off through the narrow sea between the mainland of the Troad and the isle of Tenedos—shelter and harbour of the Greek fleet in the Trojan war—then across the entrance to the straits, rounding the peninsula to go ashore at Samothrace, the island whose high snow-covered ridge seen above the drooping sky line of the Gallipoli ridge was a familiar vision to dwellers at Chanak after the Armistice. From Samothrace through the channel between Thasos and the mainland they arrived at Neapolis where they landed to enter one of the great Roman roads, the Via Egnatia.

The Via Egnatia was a highway between Rome and Constantinople and Asia minor. The Appian Way led to Brundisium (Brindisi), where the traveller took ship across the Adriatic to land at Dyrrhachium (Durazzo) and proceed by Thessalonica to Philippi for Neapolis and the Aegean, or through Thrace to Byzantium (after A.D. 324 known as Constantinople) on the Bosporus. Philippi, ten miles from Neapolis, was, as its position indicates, a city of strategic importance in the Macedonian Empire of Philip and Alexander and was equally so in the succeeding Roman empire. It was situated on a spur of the Pangaeus mountain range, which dominates the coast from near Neapolis to Amphipolis on the west. Between Philippi and the modern Drama (Drabiscus) stretches the eastern flank of the great plain where Brutus and Cassius were defeated in the famous battle of 42 B.C. which left Octavian (afterwards the Emperor Augustus), Antony and Lepidus joint rulers of the Roman world—a struggle which in Shakespeare's *Julius Caesar* has an immortal portrayal. Augustus became the sole master or *Imperator* of what was henceforth to be known as the Roman Empire in the year 30 B.C., and during his reign in 4 B.C. Jesus was born, and, a few years later, Paul. From A.D. 14 to 37 Tiberius was emperor, to be succeeded by Caius (Caligula) who died in 41. When Paul entered Philippi, Claudius had been emperor for eleven years and in 54 was succeeded by Nero. Two events took place during the reign of Claudius of quite different significance, which in this digression are worthy of mention. Paul was to meet before long at Corinth, Aquila and Priscilla, two Jews who had come there in 52, owing to an edict of Claudius which banished the Jews from Rome. This was withdrawn in 54, that is, in the last year of the emperor's life. The other event was the invasion of Britain. In 43 Claudius captured the town of Camelodunum (Colchester), and as a result the southern half of England was made a Roman province, and in half a century England, though not Scotland and

Ireland, was conquered, and for two and a half centuries was under the Empire. Christianity penetrated this remote land and established itself so firmly that it did not die out under the Saxon invaders who were converted to the faith, with the result that England, and later Scotland and Ireland, became countries in which Christianity was the religion of the people, lords and kings.

Such an excursion into contemporary history may be found useful, and, even if the facts are familiar, may serve as a reminder that Paul now finds himself in a Roman city of considerable importance, the 'first of the district' in the sense that it was the first to be reached after leaving Neapolis in that part of the wide-stretching Province of Macedonia and a 'colony'—the only place in the Acts to be so designated, though this technical term has already occurred in our account of several of the cities visited by Paul. Let us note once more that it is used of a city (not a country for which the Roman term would be 'province'), to which a body of Roman citizens were sent, usually veterans of the army whose term of service had expired, to become the governing class with officials elected by the senate known as *duumviri* who sometimes adopted the more honorific title of *praetores* (A.V. and

R.V. 'magistrates') as they did at Philippi—one of those details which mark the accurate historian who now reports the experiences of the apostles with a vivid touch all his own. Note also the presence of lictors bearing *fasces* (an axe in a bundle of rods). Philippi was a centre where Roman law and institutions, religious as well as political, were established. Nothing remains to-day to attest its former greatness; it was a hill-town watered by many streams and therefore known as *Crenides* originally (compare our own 'Wells'), and with vineyards and orchards. We are fortunate to have Paul's own letter to this church, a favourite with most readers not only because of its revealing touches about the individual members of the church but because of its lofty ethical tone and the charm of the writer's personal confessions and unveiling of his inner life. Ignatius passed through Philippi, as we have already noted, on his way to martyrdom in Rome and he was hospitably received by the members of the Church. This we learn from an allusion in an extant letter to the Philippian church which was written by Polycarp, bishop of Smyrna, soon after the death of Ignatius in Rome. Polycarp gives sound and pointed counsels to the church, but his epistle lacks the inspiring force of Paul's, as indeed he modestly acknowledges when disclaiming for one like himself, 'the wisdom of the blessed and glorious Paul'.

Paul wrote to Philippi five years after his first memorable visit. Let us attempt briefly to visualize his experiences. Think of the first preaching service, not in a synagogue, perhaps because the Jews were not as influential or numerous as elsewhere, but in a humble dwelling, a *proseuchê*, or place of prayer by the riverside. Here among others was Lydia, a capable business woman acting as an agent for a firm of dyers in Thyatira—a firm specially noted for its purple (which may have been what we call 'scarlet'). Think of her conversion (remarkably described—'whose heart the Lord opened') and her hospitality to the travelling preachers. There is also the ventriloquist; for that appears to be the literal meaning of the phrase—'having a spirit, a Python' (*marg.* R.V.) like Pythia, the prophetess of Apollo at Delphi. This nameless woman followed Paul and his friends and caused annoyance to them until, at length, she came under the power of a spirit more potent and ennobling than that to which the Delphic oracles were ascribed. Think of the protest in the forum by her angry masters and its result, the illegal beating and imprisonment of Paul and

Silas, both Roman citizens, whose pleas, if uttered, are drowned in the hubbub of the crowd or more probably ignored. Then remember the astonishing sequel—the earthquake which burst the mud walls and doorposts of the prison cell, the buoyant cheerfulness of the prisoners who mingled hymns of praise with their prayers, the despair of the jailor, his attempted suicide checked by the swift action of Paul, his awestruck gratitude and humility, his act of faith which resulted in his conversion and baptism, his hospitality and thoughtful attentions to the two apostles, and the family meal and the common rejoicing which gave a bright, homely and human climax to a series of astonishing events. Finally, recall the manly protest of the two imprisoned apostles against the treatment of the praetors, who probably thought that their release would be sufficient to cover their own illegal act. But no! Paul with quiet and effective emphasis insisted on their apology, not by proxy but in person. This secured, they consented to withdraw from the city, and after words of comfort to Lydia and the brethren they departed.

What was the outcome of this first preaching of Christ in Philippi? A little fellowship of remarkable women, Lydia, the ventriloquist, Euodias and Syntyche, with Epaphroditus, Clement and other fellow-workers, and households like those of the jailor and Lydia, who had come under the personal influence of the evangelists, including Timothy, who was afterwards to be sent there as his first charge, and Luke who was a guest in the house of Lydia with the others.

The travellers now follow the Via Egnatia south of the Pangaeus slopes, in a course roughly parallel with the coast, until they cross the foothills falling towards the mouth of the Struma (the ancient Strymon) which enters the Aegean after flowing round the north and west sides of the eminence on which Amphipolis stands. It was a city as important as Philippi—it is thirty miles from Philippi—and as full of historic interest. Renan describes the route as one of the loveliest of Paul's travels, the surface of the road paved with marble flags,[1] wells along the route supplied with fresh mountain streams, the heat tempered by shady trees. To-day, the city has vanished, but from its lonely site there is an entrancing vision of rugged stony mountain-slopes, of which the gloom and solitude are softened as the eye catches the gleam of the Aegean and the heights of Athos in the south-west, whose cliffs

[1] See his *Saint Paul*, p. 155. La voie romaine est formée de dalles de marbre . . .

are washed by its waves. Not far away across the gulf of Rendina Aristotle was born, but the site of Stageirus, his native town, is no longer easy to identify.

Amphipolis was a possession of Athens during the Peloponnesian war in which Thucydides, the great historian, was a naval commander, but it was captured by Brasidas, the Spartan general who lost his life in the hour of victory. Thucydides failed to relieve the beleaguered city and was banished, as he quietly reports in his own account of the affair. He admits his failure with the same frankness as that with which Horace, the Roman poet, admits throwing away his shield when fighting under Brutus and escaping with his life on the fateful field of Philippi. Amphipolis passed under the domination of the Macedonian kings, until it became Roman and in 167 B.C. was made a free city and head of one of the four divisions of Macedonia.

To wander over the ruins of this once great city which during the war was held by the Bulgarian forces, was to discover nothing but foundations of ruined walls, houses and temples, with here and there blocks of marble or sepulchral stones with Greek inscriptions. The only sign of human habitation was in the hamlet of Neohori at the foot of the hill near the River Struma. Here I was fortunate enough to see on a slab built into a house an inscription with the Greek words 'by this the believers conquer'—clearly a reference to the famous vision of the shining cross seen by Constantine when he entered Rome after the victory at the Milvian Bridge in A.D. 312 with the words: *In hoc vince*, 'in this conquer'. The cross survives the wrecks of time. Think of the dead cities of Galatia—Derbe, Lystra, Antioch of Pisidia—all gone, but Konia; and now in this Province of Macedonia, Philippi and Amphipolis—gone. But Thessalonica remains and to Thessalonica we now accompany Paul and his three companions.

We quoted Renan's description of the surface of the Via Egnatia between Philippi and Amphipolis and there is no reason to doubt its accuracy. The province was important; it was also rich, for gold and silver mines are known to have worked in that region. But apart from this, the making and maintenance of roads from Augustus onward was a duty for which special grants were made from the imperial treasury to supplement the provincial taxes. The 'curators of the roads' were state officials and we are informed that the cost of construction was at the rate of £900 per Roman mile. Great care was taken in their making and in constructing their surface 'camber' for draining. A layer of flat stones was placed on a foundation of rubble, and on this another layer of thick stones set in lime, above which was placed a shallow layer of rubble, and then came the pavement proper of silex or flint, or else irregular blocks of basaltic lava. Stone was plentiful in this hilly region, and perhaps marble from the quarries of Parium in the Troad may have reached Neapolis. These particulars are of interest to an age engaged in road-making and road-reconstruction on a large scale. The Romans made their roads to endure, and to-day it is not uncommon in tracing an old Roman road as e.g. that from Venta Belgarum (Winchester) to Sorbiodunum (Old Sarum) to find you have suddenly struck a surface of white flints after traversing a length of the old road which has been overgrown by grass or weeds. It would appear that the mark of the Roman Empire has been impressed on Britain for all time.

CHAPTER 7

THESSALONICA AND ITS SURROUNDINGS

THE Via Egnatia, after the Struma was crossed, skirted the Gulf of Rendina until it turned west to Apollonia—an extraordinarily common name (thirteen places of this name are given by Kiepert in his *Atlas Antiquus*), but we know nothing of this place or its site, which was about thirty-seven Roman miles from Amphipolis or about half-way to Thessalonica. South of the route was the three-pronged peninsula of Chalchidice with its eastern prong on the Aegean and its western on the Gulf of Salonika, the *Sinus Thermaicus* of the ancient world. North of the road at Apollonia was the great lake of Bolbe (modern Beshik), and some miles farther on another lake was reached south of Langaza and named to-day Avasil. Just beyond this point the road turned sharply south to Hortiach, a charming village lying at the foot of the tallest mountain in the neighbourhood of Salonika, Kotos, and then descended to the city which it enters under the arch of Galerius. It is the main thoroughfare of the city and thence goes direct to Monastir (Kitolia), ninety miles west, and finally reaches the Adriatic.

Thessalonica was originally named Therma because of the hot springs of the neighbourhood (one near lake Beshik on the Via Egnatia was a popular haunt of British troops during the war). It certainly soon came to be one of the great cities of the Macedonian Empire and Cassander, who married the sister of Alexander the Great in 315 B.C., gave to it her name, Thessalonica. Strabo speaks of it as the most populous city in Macedonia and the reason is obvious—its splendid harbour which made it a great port and trading centre of the Aegean. It is watered by two rivers—the Axius (Vardar) and the Haliacmon (Bistritza), the latter of which is crossed by the traveller proceeding round the base of Olympus from Thessaly. Surrounded by rocky hills, which in the light of the setting sun become a vivid red, it looks across the bay to snow-crowned Olympus and its less conspicuous fellow heights, Ossa and Pelion, a prospect of beauty in its way unmatched in the Mediterranean. It was clearly an important centre for Christianity, commanding not only the Province of Macedonia, but opening out on Aegean routes which brought the voyager to the Piraeus and Athens, while it was situated on the main route to northern Greece and to Illyricum for the Ionian Sea.

In Thessalonica the governor of the province resided, but as a free city it managed its own affairs, and entrusted the administration of order and justice to magistrates who bore the local title of 'politarchs'—a title corroborated on an inscription still to be read on a marble archway. There was a senate and an assembly of citizens which Ramsay believes to have been the *dêmos* of Luke's narrative (xvii. 5). It was before this assembly that an attempt was made by the hostile Jews to bring Paul and Silas. Their compatriots of the synagogue were here particularly active. For three weeks Paul had proclaimed his faith in a Messiah for whom suffering had been prophesied in the scriptures, and his message had brought conviction to a large number of devout Greeks and not a few of the leading women—an expression which indicates women of the higher social order. This was a notable result and it would appear to imply a visit extending beyond a term of weeks. This conclusion receives support from Paul's own words in 2 Thess. iii. 8, to the effect that he worked at his trade so that he might be independent of the support of others. So powerful was the influence of his preaching that the Jews, resenting his success, inflamed the passions of the rabble and made an attempt to bring him before an assembly of the people. Failing to find Paul and Silas in the house of their friend Jason, they dragged Jason and some of the brethren before the politarchs, protesting that the guests of Jason had turned the world upside down and had come to disturb the peace of their city. They stated that Jason had received the apostles and that the whole group of their adherents were enemies of the Emperor, had acted contrary to the imperial edicts and had transferred their loyalty to another king. The politarchs, though perplexed by the charge of treason, acted with restraint and after taking security for the good behaviour of the accused, dismissed the crowd. Nevertheless, the Christians deemed it wise to send Paul and Silas away by night to Beroea. The letters subsequently sent by Paul to the Church at Thessalonica imply that his desire to return was constantly thwarted. He had been deeply moved by the courage and faith of these new converts towards whom he felt like a nursing mother, full of tender solicitude. But 'Satan hindered' him—a cryptic expression, indicating that the attitude of the representatives of the empire had not changed towards the apostles, so that he could not deal in person with the situation created in the Church by the expectation of an immediate return of the Lord. It was not to be possible to revisit them for two or three years (1 Cor. xvi. 5–9).

Such is the familiar story. The solid result is the foundation of a Christian church which grew in numbers and importance. If in the first letter, he indicates the prevalence of the belief in an imminent return of the Lord, in the second he seeks to persuade his converts that there will be a previous apostasy accompanied by a temporary outbreak of evil and lawlessness. But there will be in the Imperial government a 'restraining' person or authority to hold it in check. These features indicate a situation peculiar to Thessalonica and not found elsewhere in Paul's experience. His interest was not in an ethical code induced by current apocalyptic hopes and fears, but in a new way of life, a calling fulfilled in the imitation of Christ: 'be ye imitators of me as I am also of Christ' he wrote later to the Christians of Corinth. Whether the letter to the Galatians or those to the Thessalonians stand first in order of composition, they are the earliest Christian documents that have reached us from the first century.

What then was history of Christianity in Thessalonica? We cannot of course relate it in detail; but here are some of the salient features and events. It became a centre of Christian life after the recognition of Christianity by Constantine and the foundation of Constantinople as the capital of the Eastern empire. The emperor Theodosius the Great (346–395) lived here for twelve years, choosing it as an outpost to repel the Goths, and was baptized here as a Christian; but his name is for ever stained by his fearful relapse into paganism when he ordered the massacre of seven or eight thousand citizens in the arena as a reprisal for riotous conduct and the public indignation aroused by his own oppressive administration of the city; for this act, it is to his credit that he prayed for pardon and performed penance. The city suffered from barbarian attacks after the departure of Theodosius, and seldom was free from terror; but during the seventh and eighth centuries it enjoyed comparative peace and in the ninth Bulgaria was evangelized by two natives of the city, Cyril and Methodius.[1] It sur-

[1] Brothers, who composed the Slavonic alphabet, used to-day, and translated the gospels into Slavonic.

vived the invasion of the Latin Crusaders and attacks from its neighbours, but in 1383 fell to the Turks, and after being ceded to the Venetians, once more came under the rule of the Turks, who left it in ruins, but later repopulated it. At the close of the fifteenth century it offered shelter to hundreds of Spanish Jews who fled thither to escape the terrors of the Inquisition, until at length they constituted the majority of its inhabitants. Thus, once more, Judaism had a footing in its former home, not, however, to remain united; for in the seventeenth century a serious secession took place resulting in a combination of Mohammedanism and a mystic or cabbalistic Judaism, and eventually in an esoteric community known as the Deummehs.

Steadily the city became subject to Greek influence and ascendancy, alternating with Turkish reactions, until, as we know, it finally succeeded in obtaining its independence with the renascence of Greece during the War. An astonishing story of constant unrest and change, as may be gathered even from this brief survey! But Christianity took root from the first, and was for centuries established in this city, and even under an Islamic régime held its own. In the war when Salonika was definitely a Greek city with a small Turkish quarter and cosmopolitan elements, in addition to the Orthodox churches, an evangelical Greek church existed, with other Christian activities. To-day, with complete religious freedom, commercially progressive and prosperous, with a rebuilt area to replace that destroyed by fire in the war, with reconstructed streets, modern housing and sanitation, it enters on a new epoch. Something of its splendid past is to be seen in its Byzantine churches, its ancient walls and citadel, its Hippodrome, the triumphal arch of Galerius, and its Via Egnatia by which Christianity reached it; but it looks now to the future as the second city of Greece, a port of supreme commercial importance for its hinterland and the Mediterranean lands and beyond, while it stands out as beautiful in its own situation and surroundings.

Thus Paul has succeeded in founding, almost immediately, Christian communities in two of the great cities of Macedonia; and we are fortunate to have documents, like the Acts and those letters of Paul to Philippi and Thessalonica, which have survived the complex changes of human history. These living documents move the spirit more potently than the material relics of the past. They bring before us the vital personality of a worker, untiring and self-forgetting, who dictated them in spare moments of his busy life, at times roused to instantaneous expression of his emotions by tidings of trouble, suspense, difficulty and defection in the ranks of the faithful. There are personal letters to Philemon of Colossae, to Timothy and to Titus, his own sons in the service of the gospel, and there are, in addition to those already mentioned to the churches we have visited, the letters to the churches in Corinth, in Rome, in Colossae and Ephesus; though, as we have noted, the last may have been a circular letter to the several churches of the Province of Asia. This group of letters known as 'the epistles of the imprisonment', because they have generally been held to have been written during his Roman imprisonment, are his latest in order of composition. In relation to the letters to Timothy and Titus, known as the 'pastoral' epistles, the question has been raised whether they are authentic writings of the Apostle, on the ground that they contain many words and expressions not elsewhere found in his letters, and further indicate an advanced stage of church organization which can only belong to a period subsequent to his lifetime. Now it is not impossible that, as his latest letters, they were subjected to editorial supervision and received some additions to the original text; but that they are substantially his is the verdict of those who find the above objections unconvincing. His Greek is conspicuous for its rich and copious vocabulary, which, if we may judge by analogy, would be more likely to expand than contract with advancing years; moreover, the words referred to are not unique in Hellenistic Greek, and for most of them parallels have been found. Nor, on examination of the content of the epistles, are the details of the inner life and official arrangements of the churches found to be such as to suggest a development inconceivable in Paul's lifetime. We have noted in the year 47 his appointment of elders in the Galatian churches; what more natural than there should emerge an individual of marked character and influence who would be called upon to act as leader or overseer (Gr. *episkopos*) of the elders (Gr. *presbuteroi*)? Or that deacons and deaconesses, godly women and widows should have been appointed to assist in other more personal duties, care of the sick and poor, instruction of the younger women and new converts? All the counsels are appropriate to an early period and suggest a natural development from humble beginnings. In the early Methodist societies leaders and poor stewards of both sexes were appointed to perform similar duties in their respective offices. We are still a long way from the subsequent developments of the episcopate and a hierarchy of the sacerdotal type, invested with spiritual authority. The picture presented is one of the primitive age of Christian community life with its individual churches or ecclesiae united by one Spirit.

By one Spirit—and 'where the spirit of the Lord is, there is freedom'. True, but Paul had learned from Rome the value of law and order. There must be nothing slack and disorderly, or loosely constructed in a Christian community. Where the atmosphere of spiritual liberty prevailed, the necessity of organization was not thereby annulled. There might be a diversity of gifts, of method, of outlook, as of spiritual capacity and attainment; but there must be a system of order, of self-discipline and mutual understanding. He had been taught the value of freedom in the *polis*, or Greek city state, but if his ecclesiae were to stand, they had to stand together, like a Roman cohort. Hence his liking for military figures, his metaphors from the soldier's calling—such as 'having done all, stand to your post', or 'standing fast in the Lord', or possibly from the stadium or arena of the amphitheatre. 'Each in his own order' (or military division) is his idea of the ranks of mortal humanity as they face the destiny of immortality revealed in Christ. And to the earthly church which prepares for this exalted destiny, his counsel is to 'stand fast in one spirit, with one soul striving for the faith of the gospel' (Phil. i. 27), while his joy was to see the 'steadfastness and solid front' (Moffat) 'of your faith in Christ' (Col. ii. 5). But love was the chief thing, and it was only through love that organization could be saved from lifeless formalism, or freedom from degenerating into licence.

CHAPTER 8

FROM BEROEA TO ATHENS AND CORINTH

PAUL and Silas were conducted by friendly Christians of Thessalonica beyond the walls, and went on to Beroea about fifty miles south-west of the city and known to-day as Verria (or Kara-ferria). It is pleasantly situated on a slope of the Bermios range in the valley of the Haliacmon. Here they found a strong community of Jews with a synagogue which, on their arrival, they entered, finding its worshippers of a gentler temperament than those of Thessalonica, and devoted to the study of their scriptures. They received the message of the apostles, showing eager interest in the new interpretation which they gave to the familiar text. Among these, and singled out for mention, were Greek ladies, 'not a few' of honourable social status, in addition to the men who were equally responsive. Unfortunately this striking success provoked the jealousy of the Thessalonica Jews who came to Beroea and stirred up the multitudes against the apostles.

As a result Silas and Timothy remained in the town, while Paul left with a friendly escort for the sea-coast. Timothy had not been imprisoned at Philippi and had probably been left there to join Paul and Silas later at Thessalonica and accompany them to Beroea. The nearest port to Beroea was Dium and there, Paul in company with his friends, boarded a coasting vessel and in due course reached Piraeus, the harbour of Athens.

Thus had Paul been led step by step, with unexpected variations of his route to where

> on the Aegean shore a City stands,
> Built nobly, pure the air, and light the soil,
> Athens the eye of Greece, Mother of Arts
> And Eloquence. . . .

But the reader must turn to Milton (*Paradise Regained*, iv. 238 f.) for the rest of his noble eulogium. Paul had not deliberately elected to make this his destination, but he now realized that it was a new opportunity for expounding, in the greatest university city of the world of his time, the faith of Christ.

It is not necessary to dwell at any length on the outward features of Athens, for these are familiar to multitudes who have never visited the city. Its supreme glory is the Acropolis, towering above the city and crowned by the Parthenon, the wonderful temple of Athena—the maiden Goddess—perhaps the noblest of antiquity, which, though a ruin, retains much of its original form dating from 480 B.C., the brilliant age of Pericles, when architecture and sculpture attained a classic perfection. Virgil's epithet 'breathing' best expresses the peculiar glory of Attic sculpture as those know who have seen the Elgin marbles, brought from Athens and placed in the British Museum. Nowhere else in the world are such miracles in stone to be seen. The Acropolis was a hill settlement when Abraham lived in Ur—about 2000 B.C., the age which takes its name from Mycenae, then the outstanding city of Greece—and round the site was built a wall of massive masonry, such as is revealed in the ruins of Troy. This oval-shaped height of limestone rock stands five hundred feet above the sea in a great plain, encircled by mountains on all sides but the south. One can but imperfectly imagine the city in Paul's day. The Parthenon would appear in its earlier beauty with the surrounding temples, the Erechtheum and Theseum and other monuments of Pentelic marble, and we would see the Propylaea, that magnificent gateway standing below the summit level, itself like a temple with its Doric columns and approached by a flight of marble steps, which may have been those constructed ten years before Paul's visit by the Emperor Caligula. Facing the entrance is the rocky slope known to New Testament readers of the Authorized Version as 'Mars Hill'. By the Greeks it was called *Areios Pagos*, because Ares, God of war, had been tried here on a charge of murder by his fellow-gods, and it came to be a court, in early times, for trying cases of homicide; as for example, Orestes, who murdered his mother and was tried before the Eumenides, the Avengers of blood, who had to be propitiated before acquittal was pronounced. Thus, from a legendary past, it became a criminal court and in course of time was a public authority for determining questions affecting public morals, religion and education. There was no reason why Paul should be brought under its jurisdiction, and therefore Dr. E. A. Gardner (*Greece and the Aegean*, p. 62) pleads that what actually happened was that Paul was taken by 'certain philosophers of the Epicureans and the Stoics' not before the Court, but 'to the top of this rock, as a secluded spot, close to the market-place where, like Socrates before him, he had "disputed daily with them that met with him".' All this is very natural. Paul had gone to the synagogue, as was his invariable custom, and being deeply moved by the evidences of idolatry all around, he had received a friendly hearing from his fellow Jews and the devout who had been attracted by their religion. But in addition he had gone into the market-place and had conversed with passers-by. Among the latter were people who loved an argument on the Socratic lines of question and answer about the chief good, the government of the world, the gods and immortality. Some of these took Paul to be a mere 'picker up of odds and ends', or a babbler with nothing worth listening to, and their question was 'What does he mean?' Others took the view that he seemed to be preaching a new religion as 'a proclaimer of foreign deities'. Which was much nearer the truth, though 'Jesus' and 'Anastasis' (Resurrection) conveyed no meaning to them. However, both combined to give him an opportunity for a reasoned statement and he spoke from the top of the rock.

Taking as his text the phrase 'to an unknown god', seen on an altar (probably so dedicated because the sacrificer could not name the appropriate deity and would not risk offending any of the deities), Paul, as he did at Lystra, proclaimed his belief in a personal God, the creator and lord of heaven and earth. He appealed here, as there, to the visible evidences of man's reverence and the religious sense (not to his being 'superstitious', a mistaken rendering of the Authorized Version corrected in the Revised Version margin, but unfortunately repeated in the text). God was not afar off. Man was limited in his earthly surroundings, but he owed his being to God and could therefore approach and find Him. Man had been ignorant of his true destiny, his mind being clouded by evil and therefore he needed a change of mind, all the more urgently since God had given the world a judge, affording proof of His true nature and power by His resurrection from the dead.

Up to this point he had been heard in silence. The Epicureans were thoroughgoing materialists, secretly ridiculing the pagan deities as outworn conventions. The Stoics on the other hand were pantheists with a rigid scheme of morals not without its appeal even to Paul. In fact it is possible that the quotation of his speech—'one of your own poets'—may be from the noble Stoic hymn of Cleanthes. to Zeus, 'for we are thine offspring', though it is more likely to come from

Aratus, a Cilician poet and astronomer, who wrote the exact words. There is a pantheistic element in the Pauline theology, and it appears here in the words, 'In him we live and move and have our being', but God for him is not an *Anima Mundi*, one with the universe and identified with it, but the self-determining, transcendent Being, whose spirit is immanent in humanity and nature.

Probably his hearers were ready to listen to an argument for immortality: had not Plato himself reasoned nobly on its behalf? but an actual historical resurrection, the resurrection of a man or of men, left them doubting or derisive. Nevertheless, some were willing to hear him again. And Dionysius, a member of the Areopagus council and a woman named Damaris, and others with them, believed.

When we consider the occasion, the audience, and the difficulty of securing a common point of approach to the greatest of all themes, the address was a triumph of tact, sincerity and conviction. And the fact remains—Christianity had received a hearing. Five hundred years later the temple on the Parthenon was to be used as a Christian Church dedicated to the divine Wisdom, like St. Sophia at Constantinople, and later to the Virgin; remains of Christian frescoes can still be seen on the west and north walls. In 1406 the Turks converted it into a mosque and erected a minaret in the north-west corner to indicate the fact. And thus in this majestic setting has been witnessed through the ages the sequence of Paganism, Christianity and Mohammedanism.

Athens was not the end of the long journey from Tarsus. If we allow a stay of some months at Thessalonica, nearly two years had elapsed since he had left Cilicia, and it was probably early in the year 51 when he reached what we may call the last stage of this eventful journey. At Beroea and Athens there had been no hostile and perilous opposition, and it was doubtless with a thankful heart, though with a sense of weakness and foreboding, that he approached Corinth, the second city of Greece, a great commercial and maritime centre lying on an isthmus between two ports—Lechaeum on the west and Cenchreae on the east—situated on the Saronic Gulf. It thus commanded two seas, both the western and eastern Mediterranean. The city lay to the north under the shadow of the towering Acrocorinthus nearly two thousand feet above sea-level. Its position gave it unique importance and it is not surprising that it became the most wealthy and prosperous city of the Mediterranean world, with splendid buildings and an immense population. In the struggle for freedom against Rome it suffered terribly, and was almost destroyed in 146 B.C., but a century later Rome made handsome reparation for this barbarous treatment by creating it as a colony, named after its restorer, Julius Caesar, *Laus Julia Corinthus*, and it became the capital of the Province of Achaia, and a centre of arts and crafts, a promoter of the Isthmian games and proverbial for its luxury and immorality. Its patron deity was Aphrodite, and her worship was the source of hideous profligacy and social demoralization. Henceforth his interest, his passionate devotion, all the resources of his intellect and all his spiritual gifts were directed to the proclaiming of Christ and Him crucified in this community, where the need of moral regeneration was so notorious and so appealing. He entered the city alone. Silas and Timothy had been left at Beroea and were not to rejoin him till later. But his reception was made happy by an event which was to bring him immediate comfort, and to be a source of strength for a considerable time in his residence in the city. He met Aquila and Priscilla who had recently come from Rome because of the decree of Claudius, who had banished all Jews from Rome. Like himself they were weavers of tent-cloth and thus the link of a common occupation contributed to their friendship, but still more the fact that they were eventually to become devoted Christians. They lived and worked together and Stalker is not exaggerating when he says that for Paul 'it was the nearest approach to an earthly home he was ever to enjoy'.

What of Corinth to-day? 'Annihilated for ever, the magnificence of Nero's Corinth lies buried beneath silent rubbish-mounds and green vineyards on the terraces between the mass of the Acrocorinthus and the shore of the gulf; nothing but ruins, ghastly remnants, destruction.' So writes Deissmann; but Paul's letters remain, letters into which he threw the strength of his tender and fiery emotions, entreating, upbraiding, persuading, expounding, all the time moving in one direction towards the goal of all his endeavours—to create the love of Christ. And therefore Deissmann adds: 'The paean of love chanted at Ephesus for the poor saints of Corinth has not perished with Corinth.' [1]

[1] See *Light from the Ancient East*, p. 399, and p. 116 *inf.*

CHAPTER 9

CITY CENTRES AND JOURNEYS BY LAND AND SEA

PAUL while at Philippi, was to write later (2 Cor. v. 14) from the depth of his soul to the Corinthian church the words, 'The love of Christ constraineth us'. Life narrows down for him and for most of us to a definite issue, as to a road hemmed in by the hills, like one of those gorges in Phrygia or in the Alps or the Peak or the Lake District where, restricted to a narrow track, the wayfarer finds himself enclosed not without a sense of security, even if there be peril in the background, with the sky overhead—the source of light by day and the mirror of stars by night. To love Christ and mystically share in His crucified life was the secret of his own strength and of the salvation of Corinth. Love was no longer to be degraded to wild unrestrained animal passion but to be sublimated to the sphere of the Spirit, where self-love merges into self-abandonment for the good of others and the redemption of mankind.

His road-travels were for the present at an end; they really ended at Dium on the Aegean; and what we are now attempting is to sketch his movements within the next six years, before the last journey of all on the most famous of all imperial roads.

At Corinth he was soon joined by Silas and Timothy, who found Paul 'constrained by the word' (note this expression once more), meaning that he was wholly absorbed in his appeals to the Jews, who resisted his teaching with insulting words. Their attitude was so uncompromising that Paul announced that henceforth his ministry would be among the Gentiles—that is the Roman *coloni* and the Greek population. Among the former, we may infer, was Titus Justus, who opened his house to Paul—an act of kindness which may have brought Paul into contact with a number of Romans. While Paul's interest was drawn to the church of Thessalonica, to which he sent his letters from Corinth, his attention was now also to be engaged with the prospects of Christianity in Rome. Perhaps his experiences at Athens had suggested to him the need of the capital of the Empire, and now these new associations with the *coloni* deepened his longing to preach the gospel there. It was from this city that he was at a later period to write his letter to the Romans, his most weighty and carefully constructed statement of the meaning of Christianity and the place of Judaism in the providential order and also in the divine purpose which from the first included the gentile world. In that letter there are many Roman names; moreover, we find in the first letter to Corinth (xvi. 17) those of Fortunatus and Achaicus. It has indeed been held that the final chapter of this Roman epistle was accidentally detached from the letter to the Ephesians, written from his Roman prison, but the suggestion, though interesting, is not convincing. Nor can the suggestion, that the place of his imprisonment was not Rome but Ephesus from which the epistle, being a circular letter to the churches in Asia, was despatched, be said to have won complete assent. Roman *coloni* were to be found in the Galatian and Asian churches and Paul must have met or heard of many in the course of his travels. Nor is it to be asserted without demur that Onesimus, the runaway slave, could never have got farther than Ephesus. The history of stowaways is against the idea, and as we have seen all roads and many sea-ways led to Rome. Probably there were some elements in the best type of Roman character that appealed to Paul. It is at least significant that two of his fellow-travellers bore Roman names, Silvanus and Lucanus.

For eighteen months in Corinth Paul conducted an untroubled and happy ministry. Crispus, head of the synagogue, and his household with many others joined the church, and even when, at the end of this time, the hostile Jews brought an ill-advised charge against Paul, it was summarily dismissed by the proconsul, Gallio, who, however, left the Jews to beat the ruler of the synagogue, Sosthenes, with complete indifference to what appeared to be an unimportant Jewish dispute. Taking with him Priscilla and Aquila, Paul sailed to Ephesus, and leaving them there, went on to Jerusalem for the feast of Passover in 52 (or 53) and then proceeded to Antioch, whence he made a visit to the Phrygian-Galatian churches and returned to Ephesus by way of the Province of Asia. These details are bare statements of his movements and reveal once more his interest in these Galatian Christians.

It becomes clear that though his interest in the Macedonian churches never waned, the city centres of Corinth and Ephesus were his chief concern during these years which preceded his final visit to Jerusalem and his arrest. A link between the two was that remarkable figure Apollos, an Alexandrian Jew, a learned and eloquent interpreter of the Scriptures from which he deduced the Messiahship of Jesus. As a valuable recruit, he contributed to the ever-spreading influence of Pauline Christianity. He came to Ephesus and then proceeded to Corinth. Luke is silent about the developments at Corinth and here we are dependent entirely on the letters of Paul. In addition to those extant, there was a previous letter (referred to in his first extant letter, 1 Cor. v. 9 ff.) in which he uttered a warning against immorality and friendship with immoral people. Part of this may indeed be found, as some believe, in 2 Cor. vi. 12–vii. 1, and there is another, containing a severe rebuke, mentioned in 2 Cor. ii. 4 and 9. These are all indications of great anxiety about the state of the Church. It was troubled by faction. Paul's authority was disputed and even disparaged. There was a case of incest which resulted in a solemn act of excommunication. Clubs abounded in the city, centres of common social, intellectual and religious interests. The mystery cults had devotees with whom Christians were in daily contact. A friendship might exist between a worshipper of Serapis and a convert of Christ. Hence there arose for many a Christian the perplexing problem as to whether meat offered at a pagan shrine or sacramental feast should be eaten by a Christian. The Christian sacrament had been invaded by division at the *agapê*[1] which preceded the celebration of the Eucharist. The rich members had feasted lavishly and taken precedence of the poor, whose hunger had remained unsatisfied. Questions of marriage and divorce arose out of the relationship of Christian and non-Christian; were such unions to be encouraged? On such questions and others concerned with the decorum of Christian worship and the possession of abnormal gifts such as speaking with tongues, the Apostle uttered authoritative and weighty counsels which have to be estimated in the light of the actual social questions prevailing in Corinth. He speaks with forbearance, but also on occasion with a sternness which might be, and probably was, resented. His first letter to the Corinthian church throws a vivid light on the problems which faced an early Christian community of mixed elements, mature and immature, in a pagan environment. On the other hand, it can never be out of date, because

[1] The word, translated ' lovefeast ' in Jude xii., signifies a common feast or meal, which expressed the spiritual unity of the church.

in differing forms these problems recur and are with us to-day. The reconciliation of freedom with love is one; and Paul's verdict that love is the supreme gift of the Spirit, the key to the solution of all differences, abides for ever. Undoubtedly his counsels prevailed. He certainly did not appeal in vain for generous gifts to the poor saints of Jerusalem, either at Corinth or at Philippi. We are made to feel that there is no anti-climax to his sublime peroration on immortality beginning with the words 'This mortal must put on immortality' and ending with 'your labour is not in vain in the Lord', when he proceeds to give practical suggestions for regular giving to the collection for the saints.

Next in importance was his work in Ephesus, the famous city centre of the early Christian church in Asia Minor. It lay on the River Cayster close to the sea, though to-day its site, owing to silting, is perhaps five miles inland. Its remains, which have been carefully explored, disclose the great extent of the original foundation which could be occupied by a population of over a quarter of a million. Chief among its many fine buildings was the world-famous temple of Artemis (Diana), which brought hundreds of pilgrims from afar to worship at the shrine.

Ephesus is to-day a village lying on the abandoned site of the ancient city, and the remains of the temple are the chief attraction to the modern visitor. As a city, it differed from Corinth by being less occupied with commercial interest though equally open to communication with the world both East and West. It was the gateway to Asia and, as we have already noted, stood at the end of the great route from Mesopotamia. Her citizens were proud of her world importance and it was no mere empty boast to speak of her being a religious shrine for 'all Asia and the world', as Demetrius, the silversmith, put it. Moreover, Ephesus was more intellectual in her interests than Corinth, where the arts were held in greater esteem than pure reason. Ephesus had opened her doors to the philosopher, the religious thinker and devotee. Here Christianity was known as 'the Way', which, by the by, would appeal to Paul the traveller, and recalls also his favourite verb '*to walk*' as denoting our everyday existence and duties.

Paul was therefore welcomed as a new teacher. From the synagogue he passed to 'the school of Tyrannus', and for over two years preached Christ so that 'all they which dwelt in Asia heard the word of the Lord, both Jews and Greeks'. Equally marked was his influence within the city.

The votaries of magic burnt their immensely popular cryptic books which acted as charms and thereby threw away a fortune. Then because their trade in silver models of the temple was in danger, the silversmiths led a rising of the people against the new teacher, and the rioting went on for some hours until quelled by the City Secretary, or Master of the Rolls (archives of the city), who persuaded the people that the riot was illegal and stated that they could apply to the courts on one of the regular days. The assembly was dismissed and the result was a triumph for free speech. Christianity had obviously rooted itself in the city and district, and Ephesus was to become its most important stronghold in the empire. Later in the apostolic period the aged apostle John[1] was to inspire one of his disciples to record his reminiscences and thus perpetuate the tradition of his saintliness and intellectual power as a teacher who sought to win the Greek mind to an understanding of the Incarnation, the Word made flesh, the human divine Saviour. The Fourth Gospel is the offspring of that rich creative fellowship.

[1] The name of the existing village *Ayasoluk* (*i.e. Hagios theologos*, the title given to St. John by the Byzantine Church), perpetuates his name.

Paul left for Macedonia, and here commences what is known as his third missionary journey. He visited Philippi, Thessalonica and possibly Illyricum (Rom. xv. 19); and then went to Greece, that is Corinth, where he spent three months (Acts xx. 3). Luke was not with him and Paul being hindered by a plot of the Jews from going into Syria, returned overland through Greece to Philippi. Here he wrote his second letter to Corinth and sent it by Titus and two others (2 Cor. viii. 16–22). He had as his companions representatives of Beroea, Thessalonica, Derbe and the Asian churches, who together with Timothy were sent on beforehand to Troas, where they waited for him. After spending Easter at Philippi, Paul sailed in company with Luke to Troas, taking five days—a very long passage. The movements of the historian are interesting. It would seem as if he had been resident in Philippi for a long period, and now gladly joined Paul in his journey to Troas where they first met. We have reached April 15 in the year 57, and Paul was anxious to reach Jerusalem for Pentecost, which this year fell on May 28. On the Sunday evening there was held the Agapê and Lord's Supper, followed by a discourse from Paul lasting until midnight. A youth named

Eutychus, overcome by sleep, fell from the third story and appeared to be dead, but Paul rushed to his aid and found that he was still alive. The others had already sailed to Assos; but Paul had arranged to walk there. An interesting detail! The word translated 'afoot' (A.V.) need only mean 'by land' and therefore it is an open question whether Paul walked the distance of over twenty miles to Assos or rode a mule. It was an excursion, however taken, of wonderful interest and charm. 'Assos', says Strabo, 'is strong by nature and well fortified; the ascent to it from the sea and harbour is steep and long, so that the quotation of Stratonikos, the harper, is very appropriate:

> The nearer come, to see the sooner so
> The doom of death.'

This is Leaf's translation.[1] There is a pun, because the Greek word (*asson* = nearer) may be also translated 'to Assos': and it refers to the precipitous cliffs that guard the mole and harbour. Strabo goes on to speak of it as the residence of Cleanthes the Stoic philosopher from whom Paul may have quoted at Athens, and of a greater, Zeno, who founded the school, while greatest of all, Aristotle, came to reside here. There are

[1] See *op. cit.*, p. 289 f.

remains of a very fine city, great walls, theatre and temple, and from its site there are lovely views of the valleys of the Satnois River and the ridges running from Mount Ida on the north-east horizon. Here Paul joined the ship and coasted past the islands of Lesbos and Chios to Samos, landing finally at the Trogillium promontory on the mainland, going thence to Miletus. Once a great city but now of little importance, it was overshadowed by Ephesus about thirty miles distant. Paul, to gain time, had intended to leave Ephesus out of his itinerary, but finding himself so unexpectedly near, he sent a message to the elders of the church who thereupon came to meet him. His address is one of his most moving utterances, bearing all the marks in language and thought of genuineness. There is the undercurrent of foreboding as of impending crisis, and as we read it to-day, we join in mute fellowship of spirit with that anxious company, sorrowing most of all for the words he spake that they should see his face no more. There was a similar farewell scene when, after passing the islands of Cos and Rhodes, they landed at Tyre for the unloading of their cargo. Finally, after landing at Ptolemais to spend a whole day with the brethren, they came to Caesarea and received hospitality from

Philip the evangelist. Paul, while there, had received a warning from the Judaean prophet, Agabus, who, using the symbol of a girdle, foretold bonds and imprisonment. But it was in vain. 'I am ready not to be bound only but also to die at Jerusalem for the name of the Lord.' And to Jerusalem he went.

Here we pause. The historian is now available. The 'we-passages' have been resumed, and we have already been made to feel that a full and detailed record is in hand for these coming two years that mark the crisis of Paul's life. The reader who carefully studies the last eight chapters of the Acts finds the historian rising to his greatest literary achievement merely considered as literature. He writes without haste, for during the Caesarean imprisonment he has an opportunity of gathering first-hand material for his gospel of which he may have written the first draft, while he had an opportunity of giving full reports of Paul's self-defence in his successive appearances before the crowd, before the High Priest and Sanhedrin, before Felix the procurator, Festus who succeeded him and finally before Agrippa, the vassal king, the last of the Herods and devoted to the interests of the empire. Two incidents may be noted. Paul spoke in

Aramaic to the Jerusalem crowd assembled about the steps of the castle of Antonia, and in the uproar that followed he was rescued by the centurion and brought to Claudius Lysias, tribune of the cohort quartered there. The conversation between the two is memorable. Claudius Lysias declared that he had bought the citizenship for a great sum and Paul proudly replied 'But I was born a citizen'. In the end he made use of his birthright by appealing to Caesar and from this brilliantly composed record of trials and inquiries, we may select and close with two statements of king Agrippa, first to Paul, 'With little persuasion thou wouldst fain make me a Christian, —the reply of one not yet persuaded—and finally to Festus, 'This man might have been set at liberty if he had not appealed to Caesar'.

Paul had escaped with his life from the city, where his Lord had been crucified—the city of which He had said, as Luke reports (xiii. 33), 'it cannot be that a prophet perish out of Jerusalem'. Roman firmness and justice had saved him, and he was now to receive not only just but courteous treatment from the Roman officer, Julius, centurion of the Augustan cohort, who had to undertake the responsibility for his safe convoy to Rome. Though this is a study of

Roman roads, some reference is not out of place to his experiences on the stormy waters of the Mediterranean. They boarded a coasting boat from Adramyttium, to which port it was in all probability making a return voyage. In this event Paul would once more have reached the Troad: or, in any case have found a boat at one of the Asian ports where a ship bound for Rome would have landed them at Neapolis, or elsewhere, for the Via Egnatia and Dyrrachium on the Adriatic. But it was not to be. They reached the leeward side of Cyprus, having met contrary winds and put in at Myra on the Lycian coast, where a corn ship from Alexandria sailing for Italy was found. It is not necessary to describe the voyage in detail. Luke's narrative, that of an eye-witness, is a model of accuracy and clearness, showing a knowledge of the seasonal changes and winds, the bays and harbours of the Mediterranean, the management of a boat in an emergency such as the springing of a leak and the technical terms relating to equipment and seamanship. Apart from these qualities, he gives to the story a compelling human interest with its moments of dramatic intensity, as he depicts the crises of the voyage, and the contacts of Paul with the shipmaster, who was on board for the passage, the steersman and Julius, the centurion, and the mingled elements, the crew, soldiers and passengers. We are made to feel how minds and bodies were kept at full stretch; we hear the thud of the waves as they washed over the deck and the creaking of timbers, and we realize the horror at the discovery of the leak. Pity follows on the imagination of this crew of two hundred and seventy-six souls suffering the pangs of hunger and sickness, and swept along under sunless and starless skies, over a stretch of miserable days. At length we hear a voice—the voice of Paul raised above the storm—'Be of good cheer . . . all will be well . . . there will be no loss of life among us, only of the ship'. And he told them of his vision, and the message from the unseen, 'Fear not . . . thou must be brought before Caesar. God has given you the lives of all on board . . . Cheer up! I believe God, that it will be so.' After drifting five hundred miles for a fortnight, they see land. New problems arise. The sailors conspire to leave the ship to its fate and escape secretly by the boat. But they were circumvented by the alertness of Paul. The soldiers cut the rope and let the boat fall off. Paul, this peril overpast, orders food to be brought, and before distributing it, offered thanksgiving to God. Finally, they ran the ship on the shore with the bow fixed hard aground, while the stern was breaking under the weight of the waves. The soldiers urged that the prisoners be killed, seeing that they were responsible with their own lives for their safety. The centurion, wishing to save Paul, refused their request, and in the sequel not a soul was lost: 'they escaped all to land'.

They had reached Melitê (Malta), possibly the bay known as St. Paul's Bay on the north-east of the island. Here they were hospitably received by the native people (the word 'barbarians' means that they spoke no language but their own, and were ignorant of Greek or Latin—the term being used by both Romans and Greeks of other races than their own). The governor of the island, or deputy of the praetor of Italy, made Paul and his friends his guests for three days, honouring the apostle for his kindness to his father in sickness and for the cure he effected. Paul had escaped death from a viper's bite and was deemed to be a god. He used his gift as a faith healer with such manifest efficacy that he wrought many cures and received much honour from the healed. After three months they sailed for Italy on the *Twin Brothers* (Castor and Pollux) and after landing at Syracuse they reached Rhegium on the south-west of Italy and finally landed at Puteoli on the Bay of Naples, passing Capri, that ravishing island which was the private possession of the emperor, Augustus having exchanged Ischia to secure it. Here came Tiberius preferring it to Rome as a residence for long periods as well as short visits; and on the Monte Tiberio, where his palace was built, we see to-day the gardens of the lovely home of the author of *The Story of San Michele*. Thus, in the bay famous for its beauty, under soft Italian skies, on the fair Campanian coast, Paul's voyage came to an end. Nothing more vivid and appealing than the narrative of Luke has come to us from the classical literature of Rome or Greece, while from the background of gloom and tempest shines out the personality of Paul with his gifts of leadership, resourceful and firm, yet also patient, compassionate, self-forgetting, without fear and without reproach.

CHAPTER 10

BY THE VIA APPIA TO ROME

THE *Twin Brothers* landed her passengers and cargo at Puteoli, on the Bay of Naples, one hundred and forty-one miles from Rome. In the classical age Puteoli had as its neighbour on the eastern side Baiae, the famous pleasure resort, where the *élite* of Rome had country houses. In the early empire both places were connected by a causeway of earth and stones. Puteoli was then the naval base or Portsmouth of Rome; for Ostia, the port of Rome, at the mouth of the Tiber was not suitable for any but trading and coasting ships. Marcus Agrippa, counsellor and friend of Augustus, and gifted with a brilliant organizing genius, saw that it was fitted by nature to be the headquarters of the imperial navy. Near at hand were two inland lakes, the larger, Avernus, and the shallower between it and the sea, Lucrinus. These two he connected with a channel which could be entered by ships of war from either end of the mole which connected the two towns. Thus was formed the famous harbour called Julian after the imperial family and referred to by Virgil in a famous passage (Georgics ii. 161–4). Puteoli was noted, too, for its volcanic soil which when mixed with lime, formed the *pozzolana*, a cement of marvellously enduring quality. 'This concrete became for the Roman people what the steel frame is for us of to-day.' [1] It is because of the inner core of this cement that the ancient buildings of Rome whether faced by stone, marble or brick, have remained till to-day.

But in this region nothing was secure. In 1538 an earthquake raised the level of the Lucrine Lake and destroyed all traces of the famous *portus Julia*. More familiar is the terrible eruption of Vesuvius which overwhelmed, in the year 79, some twenty years after Paul's landing at Puteoli, the coast towns of Pompeii and Herculaneum. Warning of this event had been afforded sixteen years before, when Vesuvius, until then quiescent with its green covered slopes rich in vineyards, discharged lava and dust into the streets of Pompeii, a splendid city, of which the main features, streets, temples, theatre, forum, houses, have been brought to light after eighty

[1] See *Marcus Agrippa*, by F. A. Wright, p. 129.

years' work—a restoration without a parellel in history.

These are some of the memories which the sight of the modern Puzzuoli recalls, although, unlike Pompeii, its original features have disappeared. Paul had the joy of being welcomed to the land he had longed to visit by Christian brethren—a notable fact. For neither Paul nor Peter can be claimed as pioneers of the faith in Italy, nor indeed at Rome. Neither can they be described with any certainty as founders of the Christian church in Rome. These brethren who welcomed Paul were Christian Jews, but we cannot rule out the possibility that among them were those who, originally pagans, had through Judaism become attached to the new faith.

After leaving Puteoli the traveller crosses the rich Campanian plain to Capua, where he is on the main Appian road. Capua was a city of great importance, so much so that the Gate from which the road commenced at Rome was named the Porta Capena; and as having in the Punic war been actually held by Hannibal, the Carthaginian general, it was associated with a never-to-be-forgotten crisis in the history of the Republic. Strabo calls the Via Appia 'the queen of great roads'. It is certainly one of the oldest and most travelled, as it connected Rome with Brundisium, on the Adriatic, the port for Macedonia and Greece. We have an entertaining account of the journey to Brundisium by Horace, the Roman poet, in the Satire (i. 5), where he describes his experiences in company with a learned Greek rhetorician. Arrived at Capua from Puteoli, the convoy in charge of Julius turned sharply to the west and reaching the coast passed the towns of Sinuessa, Minturnae (Minturno), Formiae (Formia) and Fundi (Fondi), a favourite resort of Cicero, near which he was assassinated, until they reach Anxur (Terracina), set on its white gleaming rocks, as Horace describes it. At this point the road, running perfectly straight in the true Roman fashion, crosses the Pomptine marshes, an unhealthy region, where a canal or wide drain was made by Augustus, as an alternative to the road which ran near it. At length the town of Appii Forum was reached, where Horace spent a restless night from mosquitoes and noisy frogs among inhabitants far from reputable or attractive. Ten miles onward they came to Tres Tabernae, a village at which a road from Antium, an important coast town, converged, and here Paul had the joy of being welcomed by a company of Christians who had travelled to meet him. If his heart had hitherto failed in moments of depression as he drew near to the city of destiny, he now 'took courage'—a happy touch that reveals the eye-witness, his fellow-traveller, Luke. Aricia, sixteen miles from Rome, was next reached. Paul was now on the slopes of the Alban Mount, the range of hills where to-day suburbs such as Frascati, attract the city dweller. Near Rome the Appian Way is lined by tombs, not all of which existed in Paul's day. That of Cecilia Metella, familiar to the modern sightseer, had recently been erected and from this commanding point, Paul could look back on the hills, among which he had come so far and see before him the road on which, according to the legend, Peter, fleeing from Rome, met Christ and cried 'Lord, whither goest thou?' and heard Him say, 'I go to Rome to be crucified' . . . 'and Peter came to himself and returned to Rome'.[1]

The Via Appia in the early empire entered the city by the slopes of the Caelian Hill through the Porta Capena, the site of which was discovered in the ancient wall of Servius Tullius, from which point under the Palatine hill the traveller would reach the entrance to the Via Sacra. But no arch of Titus (nor of course the arches of Septimius

[1] See Acts of Peter, *Apocryphal N. T.*, James, p. 333.

Severus or Constantine), and no Colosseum were then to be found; yet many an archaeologist would like to have a glimpse of the Forum as Paul saw it, with its splendid columns, temples and palaces, mostly to-day in ruins. Here too he might have used his Athenian epithet and called the Romans 'most-religious', but in the sense attaching to a worship of the gods associated with a system of feast-days (*fasti*) for the glorification of the Genius of Rome.

'And so we came to Rome' . . . writes Luke simply, but with an undercurrent of pride. Through the Capene Gate had gone in years past a host of distinguished and obscure people, kings, generals, ambassadors, prisoners and captives, but none like Paul, whose achievement was to be a builder of a world religion, upon the one foundation, which is Christ.

Paul was no ordinary prisoner, as Julius, the centurion, had long ago discovered. His splendid courage, his cheerfulness in mortal peril, his extraordinary gifts which had so marked a psychic effect on his fellows, all these had impressed him and in handing the prisoner over to the officer of the Praetorian guard he could and doubtless did bear testimony to these qualities. All that we know is that Paul had permission to live in his own lodging under the supervision of a soldier, to whom he was attached by a light chain. For two years, 60–62, he had a reasonable amount of liberty. Three days after his arrival, he met the leading Jews and stated to them his view of the new gospel. 'Some believed and some doubted'; but nothing daunted 'with all confidence' (*parrhêsia* [1] a favourite word of his), 'no man forbidding him', he preached the kingdom of God and taught about the Lord Jesus Christ. A splendid finish to the finest travel book that had been yet produced in the empire! There is no need to think of it as an unfinished record; it is better to believe that we have it as it left the hands of Luke.

What happened next? A new chapter has opened, the content of which is largely conjecture. But we cannot doubt the evidence of 2 Timothy iv. It has the ring of a personal and authentic farewell message. He had been brought up for examination and been acquitted, 'delivered from the mouth of the lion'. If this is so, we cannot pass lightly over the tradition that he carried out his purpose to go to Spain. He would go either by sea or by the Via Aurelia to Massilia (Marseilles) along the Côte d'Azur and thence into Spain. All is of course conjecture, but there can be little doubt

[1] See *Studies in the Language of St. Paul*, p. 48 f.

about the tradition that he was beheaded later in the year A.D. 64 during the terrible persecution under Nero—beheaded with the sword, because he was a Roman citizen and not treated as Peter was, or as Ignatius was destined to be, with the indignity of a common criminal, the one crucified and the other the victim of the beasts of the arena. There are traditions that his execution took place at Tre Fontane, where the abbey of that name was built as a chapel of the Basilica of 'St. Paul beyond the walls', and further, that the bodies of St. Paul and St. Peter were placed before burial in the church of San Sebastiano. During recent excavations in this church a staircase was discovered descending to what may have been the temporary resting-place of their bodies. This church stands on the Appian Way, and beneath it are catacombs where the early Christians were buried.

We learn from the second letter to Timothy that Paul was not alone, when the end was drawing near. Silas passes out of the record in Acts xviii. 5, left at Corinth with Timothy. Timothy was with the apostle in Rome; his name appears in the greetings sent to the churches of Philippi and Colossae; but he is away when the second letter to him was written, and Paul urges him to come at once and bring Mark with him. The last we hear of him is in the epistle to the Hebrews xiii. 23, where his release from imprisonment is announced, showing that he may have been put into prison when visiting Paul on the eve of his execution. Paul had urged him to bring his cloke (a travelling outer garment with a hood) and 'the books', together with the vellum copies,[1] which were the more valuable. Titus, Crescens and Tychicus were with him; while Eubulus, Pudens, Linus and Clauda with all the brethren join in the greetings of this second letter to Timothy. Interesting names—most of them Roman ; one wonders if Linus was the first bishop of Rome, bearing that name. Luke too was by his side: he may be—he deserves to be—'the brother whose praise in the gospel is spread through all the churches' (2 Cor. viii. 18). What a host of friends the apostle had gathered round him in his travels. And now the travels were nearly over. How fitting from the wayfarer is his word 'The time of my departure is come'. The word is the familiar English 'analysis'; but in the Greek it means the departing from a temporary resting-place or khan. It is a traveller's word, and suggests a further journey, another setting-

[1] Probably rolls of the Old Testament are indicated by the original *membrana*, a parchment made at Pergamum.

out, and for him something far better, the adventure of the unseen world. We have in imagination shared his company on two continents. There is no record of his having reached Egypt or north Africa—regions where Christianity was for generations to achieve so great a triumph. Could he have looked into the future, he could have repeated with a larger vision and assurance than was possible in the first century the assertion that 'the gospel was in all the world bearing fruit and increasing'. Nevertheless, his spirit and his gospel are needed more than ever to-day. If that for which he laboured with single-minded devotion is to be brought to perfection, it is for us to draw our inspiration from the same source of power, the power of 'him that is able to do exceeding abundantly above all that we ask or think', whereby in weakness he was made strong throughout his service for the kingdom of God. Therefore he could say with the humility of one who did not count himself to have apprehended, and yet with the full assurance of faith:

> 'I have fought the good fight,
> I have finished the course,
> I have kept the faith :

henceforth there is laid up for me the crown of

righteousness, which the Lord, the righteous judge, shall give to me at that day, and not to me only, but to all them also that have loved his appearing' (2 Tim. iv. 7–8).

GENERAL INDEX

(r. = river, s. = sea, l. = lake, m. = mountain)

INDEX

INDEX

INDEX

INDEX

E.N.A. Photo

The Cilician Gates through the Taurus Mountains.

Frontispiece

(*a*) Konia (Modern).

Plate 2

(*b*) The Acropolis of Konia, showing Mosque of Alau-ed-Din, turret of Church of St. Amphilochius appearing on the left and Karatai Mosque and marble doorway in the foreground.

Sirtchali Medresseh, a School of the Seljukian era, Konia.

Court of Seljuk Khan, Konia.

(*a*) Tomb of Seljuk Sultan: Akshehr (Philomelium).

(*b*) River Scene, Akshehr (Philomelium).

Ancient Khan near Ishaklu on the north road through Phrygia, with a mosque turret in the background.

Gate of an ancient Khan near Tchai (Julia Ipsus) on the road to Akroenus (Afium-Kara-Hissar).

Plate 7

(*a*) View from the Citadel of Afium-Kara-Hissar.

(*b*) The Citadel Rock of Afium-Kara-Hissar.

Plate 8

(*a*) Kutahia: Citadel.

(*b*) Eskishehr.

Plate 9

Phrygian Tomb, at Deuver near Eskishehr.

(*a*) The Hill of Troy from the plains showing the gap made by Schliemann in his first excavation and Turkish trenches at the base.

(*b*) Mycenaen Walls, Troy.

Plate 11

(*c*) The Road to the Hill of Troy showing ancient stairway on the left.

(*a*) The Harbour of Alexandria Troas: Tenedos in the distance.

(*b*) Kavalla, formerly Neapolis.

Imperial War Museum Photo

Looking from above on the site of Amphipolis in foreground, with the Struma at the base and with the Range of Bunar Dagh (Pangaeus) in background.

(*a*) Macedonia. Stone-breakers on the road to Salonika from Hortiach, Mount Kotos in the background.

Plate 14

(*b*) Salonika looking towards the west from the air.

(*a*) Church of the Prophet Elias, Salonika.

(*b*) Church of the Holy Apostles, Salonika.

(*a*) The Arch of Galerius, via Egnatia.

(*b*) Verria (Beroea).

Alinari photo

(a) Athens. The Acropolis with a panoramic view of the city.

W. F. Mansell

(*a*) Athens. The Areopagus (Mars Hill), from which Paul addressed the crowd drawn from the market-place, consisting of Stoics, Epicureans and others.

(*b*) Assos: View to the north-east from the summit.

Anderson photo.

The old Appian Way near Rome.

9 781532 635038

www.ingramcontent.com/pod-product-compliance
Lightning Source LLC
LaVergne TN
LVHW010932100826
845153LV00001B/12
9781532635045